A Whisper in the Wind

RUTH INMAN

WESTBOW
PRESS®
A DIVISION OF THOMAS NELSON
& ZONDERVAN

WestBow Press books may be ordered through booksellers or by contacting:

WestBow Press
A Division of Thomas Nelson & Zondervan
1663 Liberty Drive
Bloomington, IN 47403
www.westbowpress.com
844-714-3454

ISBN: 978-1-6642-1472-9 (sc)
ISBN: 978-1-6642-1471-2 (e)

Print information available on the last page.

WestBow Press rev. date: 12/02/2020

This story is dedicated to two ladies who greatly influenced my life –
My mother, Ethel Goodwin Cooke, and my mother-in-law, Bertha
Rackley Inman. Both women were wonderful Christian women
who reached out to people in need whether they were neighbors or
strangers.

A special thanks to Rev. Dean Parker and Rev. Ernie Barrentine
for their help in bringing this book into being. Without their help
there would be no book.

I hope that everyone that reads this story will be moved to get
out of their comfort zone and help someone that is in need.

Ruth Inman

*I would like to say thank you to my
granddaughter, Ashley Homer, she really
did a great job on the cover for my book!*

RUTH

ONE

IT IS EARLY IN the morning and the sun can be seen peeking over the horizon. It is a warm spring day. April in the South has always been my favorite time of the year. As I drive along 1-95, my mind drifts back to the life I am leaving behind.

I was born Gayle Hendricks, and I grew up in a very close family with two brothers and one sister. My parents raised us well. Mother, who I adored, was a wonderful Christian woman and my father taught us what hard work was and gave us good guidelines to follow.

I attended a very small school, so I practically knew everyone. I was not the most popular girl around, but I had three close girlfriends. I didn't have many boyfriends. There was one named Tony that I liked. He was so sweet and popular but he never asked me out. I was very shy then and kept to myself most of the time.

After graduation, I had numerous jobs, none of which I really enjoyed. That is the reason I am leaving today. Saying goodbye to Mama and Daddy was not easy. I wanted to cry. Mama told me what she has always told me – to follow my heart and to listen for the whisper in the wind.

It is about lunchtime, and I better get off at the next exit and get something to eat. I also need to get some gas. I found Wendy's will do just fine. When I go in, I notice the line is very long, so I will have plenty of time to decide what I want to eat. I got my food and found a place to sit by a window. The food was very good, but it was very loud with lots of little children running and playing. I would like to have some children one day, after I spread my wings a little.

Some man is staring at me with a grin on his face. I sure do hope he doesn't come over here. He got up and moved closer to me. I ate my last few bites and dumped my tray. I made a mad dash to the car. He came out right behind me and got in his truck, he is driving an awful green truck that looks like it is about a sixty-nine Chevy. Lord, please don't let him follow me. I've looked back a few times and haven't seen him anywhere. Thank goodness!

I have always dreamed of going to New York, I can't wait to get there. I have a very long drive ahead of me, and I do not want to be driving when it gets dark. The radio is playing and I am relaxed now, I don't feel so tired. I have been driving for a long time. I need to stop and find a place to stay for the night. I see a Comfort Inn off the next exit that will be good. I went in and got a room, got my key, the room was very nice and looked very clean. I took a hot shower and went to bed.

I woke up around eight, got dressed and went down stairs. I grabbed a cup of coffee in place of breakfast. I got my things together and got back on the road. I am so excited, can't wait to see New York.

I drove about all day, stopped a few times for a bathroom break, and to get a bite to eat. It is about two o'clock in the morning, guess I should stop for the night. I am not very far from the big city. I need to call Mama and let her know that I am okay. I found a nice motel, went in, and got a room. I found a pay phone so I can call Mama. She will accept a collect call. "Mama, hey, it's me. Are you alright?" She was so happy to hear my voice. "Honey, I am fine. How are you?" I told her that I was tired but okay. She told me again how proud she and Daddy were. We talked for a few more minutes then said goodbye. I assured her that as soon as I got settled in at my new place that I would call and give them the details.

I went back up to my room. It feels strange to be so far from home and from my family. I know it will be a big adjustment for me. I opened the blinds over the window so that I could see all of the tall buildings against the horizon. I took a bath and went to bed. I had trouble getting to sleep; too much to think about. I woke up early, thinking about all that I needed to do today. I am close enough to the big city. I need to leave everything here and go out and see if I can locate a job.

After I got dressed, I hit the streets. I left my car and decided to walk. This way I could be sure not to miss any opportunities that may arise. The air is thick and looks like smoke. I guess that is what they call smog. I spotted a bookstore up ahead and decided to walk in and ask if they needed any help or if they knew anyone looking for help. I went in and this middle-aged gentleman came up to me, "May I help you, young lady?" I asked if he needed any help in the store. He smiled and told me that he was not hiring right now. I left the store and went further down the street. People were bumping into me and pushing me; I can't believe the way it is here. Lord, what a crowded place. I had to remind myself that this is what I wanted. I guess I must have been deranged.

There's a small dress shop. I'll just go in and charm them. As I passed the window, I caught a glimpse of a green truck going down the street. "No, it can't be the same one I saw when I was at that restaurant on the way here." I ran in the store and peeked out the window. It was gone. "Miss, are you alright?" I turned and this nice looking lady was smiling at me. "Yes, I am okay. I just thought I recognized someone, that's all." "Well then come on in and look around for a bit," she said. "Maybe you will find yourself a nice dress." "No, thank you, but I am looking for a job. I just moved here from South Carolina. I also need a place to live." "My dear, you are in luck, because I need someone to help me. Have you had any experience in clothing sales?" she asked. "When I was in high school I worked at a retail store. I will try very hard to learn if you will give me a chance." "Come over here and fill out these papers and we'll talk." I sat down and filled in the blanks. I just could not get the image of that truck out of my mind. Surely, it was only a coincidence; that could not have been the same truck.

I got the job. I does not pay much but maybe enough to survive until I can do better. The manager, Selene, was very nice. I wonder where he last employee was and why she left. Maybe I am just too suspicious or something, who knows, time will tell. She mentioned that there was a garage apartment for rent near where she lived. I will surely go and look at it tomorrow. Selene asked me to open the store for her at nine and to leave around five. This is a big responsibility, but I really must do this.

Selene is showing me the ropes so to speak. I don't go in until ten today, that way I will be able to check out the apartment she told me about. I got in my car and followed the directions Selene had written out for me. Go five blocks east, turn left onto Cherry Drive. I didn't have a hard time finding the apartment. The yard is small but that won't matter. The lady that owns the apartment lives next door. I went over and talked to her. She was nice but picky; the rent was $150.00 a week. I asked her why it was so much with only one bedroom, a small kitchen, and a small bath. "This includes your water and also your lights," she said. "Oh, I'm sorry. I didn't know. That's really not bad at all. I'll take it!" She wanted a month's rent in advance. Now I have almost spent all the money I had saved up. I explained that I had to work and that I would not be able to move in until tomorrow. I paid her and went back to the motel. I am surely about broke now. I hurried to get dressed and rushed off to work.

"Selene, the apartment is great! I took it, thanks!" She was just quietly going about the store. I asked her what was wrong, but she always tells me that she is fine. I can feel that there is something just not right. I have been known to be a little nosey, so maybe I will find out.

I closed the store, I went back to my motel room and began packing for the move. I finished about eleven thirty. I was very tired, so I took a quick shower and went to bed. My alarm clock woke me at six in the morning. "I am moving today," I said aloud. "God, thank you for bringing me this far safely. I am so thankful." The car is packed and my bill is paid; now to my new apartment I go. I drove up the driveway beside the garage stairs. It's about ten o'clock. I have the rest of the day to get settled in. I have never liked stairs but this is the way it is. Dragging my luggage up the steps, I stopped to look around at my surroundings. The houses nearby are so close to each other, but they have very neat yards. There is a soft breeze blowing today and plenty of sunshine. There is a big oak tree right beside my porch. I can hear the birds singing in the trees. Maybe all this is a good sign. I just feel so good about my life right now. "God, thank you for your guidance," I said aloud. I looked down to see my landlord, Mrs. Pearson, staring out of her kitchen window. I waved and she smiled and waved back. Mrs. Pearson was widowed and now lived alone. She was about sixty years old. She must have enough money, she doesn't work anywhere, I thought. Maybe I will be that lucky one day.

It's getting dark, I've got to get something to eat. I walked across the back yard to Mrs. Pearson's house. I knocked on the door. "Hi, Gayle, are you settled in?" "Yes, ma'am. I just wanted to know where the nearest supermarket is. I need to get a few things." She smiled and gave me directions to the Food-mart. It was about half a mile away. I was praying all the way not to get lost. The traffic is so thick and moves so fast, if you miss your turn you will have to go a long ways to turn around. I got there without a hitch and found what I needed. When I got to the register, the line was very long. While waiting, I looked up at the mirror hanging from the ceiling. "Oh, Lord," I thought. That man looks like the driver of the green truck. No, it can't be him. I must stop thinking that I see him all the time. I don't know why, I just feel a sense of fear. I don't want to stare, but I can't help but wonder if this man has really followed me here. I paid for the food and hurried to my car. I am beginning to think I am insane. I don't see him anywhere or the green truck.

TWO

I MADE IT BACK to the apartment safely and put away the food. I ate a frozen pizza and soon went to bed. I can see the moonlight shining softly through the blinds. As I lay here, I am amazed at how big the world is and that the same moon is shining on my family back home. I don't have a telephone yet. I need to call Mama tomorrow. I know she is praying for me and this really gives me peace.

Tomorrow is Sunday and I don't even know where a church is. Maybe I can ask Mrs. Pearson in the morning. I slowly drifted off to sleep.

I woke up around eight thirty. I guess I was more tired than I thought. I went to the window. Mrs. Pearson's car was still at home. I wondered if I should go over or not. Does she even go to church? I know Mama would want me to go to church, so I took a deep breath and went to her back door. I knocked. I could see her at her table reading the paper. She came to the door. "Hi, sorry to bother you again, but I just wondered where the nearest church is?" She looked very pleased. "About two blocks down. You can see the steeple. It's a nice Baptist church. It's called Westminster Baptist Church. The people are very nice. I haven't been in a while but I'm not much for going by myself. Since my husband, Robert, died, I haven't been very many times." "Would you like for us to go together?" I asked. "I can drive if you show me the way." She looked so pleased. "I don't want to impose on you but that would be nice."

We went to church together that day and that really started a wonderful friendship between us. She invited me to go every Sunday with her. She insisted that I call her by her first name, Maeta. I asked if I could call her Mama Maeta. She seemed pleased with this. I guess she sort of adopted me since she had no children of her own. It really felt good to have her close to me. It sort of filled the big gap in my life. I really missed my Mama and Daddy.

After a while, work at the store seemed to consume my life. I hoped to meet some young people my age to go out with. There was a very nice man at church that Mama Maeta had introduced me to. His name was Patrick Thomas. He was a business executive for the LoBo Toy Company in downtown New York. He was friendly but I felt really dumb around him. There I was, a little southern girl, working in a dress shop and he was so educated. I was hopeful that maybe one day he would ask me out.

Much to my surprise, sure enough, on Friday afternoon I looked up and there was Patrick standing in the shop. "Hi," he smiled, "working hard?" "No not really, how are you?" "I am doing fine, I would like for you to have dinner with me – this would make me feel even better", he smiled. "I would like to. I get off at six but I'll need to go home and change." "No let me pick you up here. You look just fine" he replied. I locked the store and Patrick and I went to dinner at a little deli on the corner of 23rd and Smithwood. It was nice, the food was great and so was my friend. We talked a lot about work, somehow I felt an easiness between us. It was really strange since we really just met. I found out that he was born and raised in Ashville, NC, and that he worked his way through college. He sent to North Carolina State and majored in business administration. He worked small jobs at first and with a run of good luck, landed the job in New York, and has been there for the last four years. He told me about this humble upbringing, working along beside his father building houses. He is 25 and has never been in a serious relationship. We talked until 11:30 pm. He drove me back to my car and waited until I got in and said "I'll call you at work tomorrow." He waved and smiled. He sat there and watched me drive away. All the way home I thought this is too easy, he was actually nice and also cute – too cute. I unlocked my door, kicked off my shoes, and got a cup of coffee. I sat on the bed thinking maybe my life is off and running now.

Patrick and I see each other off and on. We have fun but nothing serious yet.

Selene opened up the store today like usual. When I got there she was very quiet. Doesn't she know that when she is this way I worry about her? She would barely answer yes or no questions. "Selene, we need to talk, what is wrong?" She went to the bathroom. I could hear her vomiting. I was so scared that something would happen to her. What in the world can I do? I don't know her family, she never talked about them. I think, yes, she mentioned a married sister that lives near here. "Selene," I yelled through the door, "please let me call someone. Please let me call your sister. You seem so sick." "No," she yelled back through the door. "No, no, no!" Then I heard her fall. I forced open the door. She was laying on the floor, white as a sheet and washed down in sweat. I ran to the telephone, call 911, and then ran back to her. Why didn't I realize before now that she was sick, not just quiet?

After the ambulance left with her, I went through her phone book looking for some sort of information about her sister. I found a picture of a woman that looked like Selene. Could this be her sister? I looked at the back of the photo. Susanne Palmer was written on it. There was a date and also an address. What do I do? I called Patrick and filled him in. He drove up to the store. We called every Susanne Palmer in the telephone book. On the third try, we hit pay dirt! She said she was Selene's sister. I tried not to scare her too much. She was grateful that I called. I asked what I should do with the store tomorrow. She suggested I open it at ten and close at four. That way I would not get so tired.

Selene was very sick. I visited her at the hospital almost every day. I found out that she had cancer. It was in the last stages. It was in her liver and probably throughout her body.

I met Susanne and her husband, Ray. He seemed a little weird at times but Susanne really seemed to be nice. Every time I am in Ray's presence, I feel like he is undressing me with his eyes. I really hate that feeling.

Now I understand why Selene always worried about money all the time. She never wanted to buy new styles of clothes for the store. Now I understand why. She was probably afraid that she would not be around to pay the bills.

I worked in the store five hours a day. I didn't really like being in the store alone but I stayed busy. We had a lot of young people that shopped with us. The girls were always friendly. This helped pass the time. I don't go out with Patrick much now. I am always so tired and I try to go and see Selene every day. She talked to me today and cried a lot. Ray and Susanne were there. He still stares at me.

I stayed a little while and left. She was not doing well. The doctor said her liver and kidneys were in real trouble. She didn't seem to care if she died. I could tell by the way she acted that it really did not matter to her. The doctor said by the time she was diagnosed, it was too late for any kind of treatment. I prayed every night that God would give her the strength to pull through this. I talked at great length with my Mama and also with Mama Maeta about her. They both said that God would probably be very kind to her and let her die; therefore, no more pain.

At the hospital today the doctor told us that Selene went into shock, and that her kidneys have shut down. Her breaths have gotten short and very labored. As I stood by her bed side, I thought what a waste. She was such an attractive woman and was only thirty eight years old. God I stand here so helpless, she is going to die. I do not know what to say to her sister, Susanne. She told me Selene had always been a loner, no friends. That is the night that she passed away. I cried and cried. Patrick came over to my apartment and stayed with me until I could get myself together.

He went with me to the memorial service. It was a very simple service. "Patrick, I didn't ask Selene if she was a Christian or not. What if she wasn't?" Patrick tried to make me feel better. I have such a guilty feeling about this. I promised God that I would make up for that somehow, some day.

Susanne told me that she had decided to sell the store. Now what in the world was I going to do? I was out of a job now. Susanne and I went through the stock at the store. It took us about a week to access the value of everything. She apologized for my dilemma and said she needed the money to pay Selene's bills. I assured her that I understood. After that day, I rarely saw her. I had really grown to like her, but Ray, he was a different story.

Patrick told me that a friend of his at work knew a girl at the hospital. She had often talked about people being able to go to nursing school through the hospital. He gave me her name. She was an LPN. I called her. She told me to meet her today. She told me about a program they have where I could work and go to school. I would need to sign a contract with the hospital for at least three years. I told her that I would need to think about it for a few days. She agreed to wait four days. That would be this coming Monday. Me, a nurse, I do not know about that.

THREE

WHEN I GOT HOME, I called my Mama and told her about the idea. She was really happy, she yelled out to my Daddy, "Our girl is thinking about going to be a nurse. What do you think about that?" She said that he smiled and said "Tell her to go for it if that is what she wants to do." We talked for a little while longer and then said our goodbyes.

I went over to Mama Maeta's house, I am behind on my rent. I told her about my idea and asked if she could give me a little more time to catch up on the rent. She was so kind. She just smiled, as always, and said "Gayle, you take all the time you need to decide what you really want to do." This gave me some relief. How was I going to pay the rent or eat? I surely can't get a loan on my car – it's too old. I pray that God will help me do the right thing.

I used the days to clean my apartment. It really needed it. I thought about school a lot. It felt like a dream. I go and visit Selene's grave sometimes. It is always so peaceful there. The little squirrels always play around the big oak tree that is beside her grave. The world is such a beautiful place, we are the ones that mess it up.

Mama Maeta knocked on my door. "Gayle, the mailman brought you a registered letter. I signed for it because you were not at home. I thought it might be important. I hated for him to take it back. I hope that was okay." I thanked her. "I don't think I can take any bad news. I can't take much more change." I asked her to sit down on the steps with me while I opened it. Down inside I was afraid something was wrong with Mama or Daddy. I was really afraid to open it. "Take a deep breath child and open it up." I ripped it open and inside there was a note. "Gayle, Daddy and I have prayed about your decision and God has directed us to help you the only way we can besides praying, that is. So here is a money order for five thousand dollars. We both have been saving for a long time. If you use it wisely, you can pay your bills and eat for a while. Lots of love, Mama and Daddy." Needless to say, I jumped with joy and grabbed Mama Maeta and hugged her tight. We both were so happy but felt guilty taking the money. I guess the best way to repay them is to do well and to graduate from nursing school. I will study hard and do my very best to make them glad they helped me this way.

I called Patrick and gave him the good news. He was so happy for me. I walked over to the window. The moon seemed to be extra bright tonight. I thank God for the great peace that I feel now.

The next few weeks were filled with excitement and fear all rolled into one. I contacted the hospital and told them that I was ready for school. They asked me to come up and get everything ready. I went and got all my paperwork together.

I drove over to the college. It took me about twenty minutes. Morton College is really big! I think they have about 2,000 students. That's scary. Maybe now I will meet girls my own age with some of the same interests.

School started and so far so good buy it seems like all I do is study and attend school. Patrick helps me study sometimes. I miss being with him. We don't go out very often. Sometimes we go out on Saturday night and get supper and maybe go to a movie. I still see him at church. We sit together most of the time. He would hold my hand, smile, and wink at me. Mama and Daddy write me often to encourage me. I will be so glad to be able to help sick people.

My grades are good. I have kept a "B" average. Time is passing really fast. We are working in the hospital now. We get to wear our cute uniforms. They are white with blue aprons. The hands-on training is so much fun. I really like working with the elderly patients. They have witnessed so much history. I love talking with them. I think the older ones are always going to be my favorites.

This is nearing the end of my second year. My money is really getting scarce. I talked to my counselor at school. She asked me if I would be interested in working on the weekends. This would give me some extra money. I know it will be hard but I need the money. I agreed to work. I asked if I could work at night on Sundays so that I could still attend church. The supervisor said she would try to work out the schedule that way. I know I won't get to see Patrick hardly any at all now. There is only six more months left in school, maybe I can make it. Patrick says he understands and that he will be right by my side all the way through. He is a wonderful man. I am really beginning to care a lot for him. I think the feeling is mutual.

The time has really flown by. Graduation time is here. I wanted Mama and Daddy to come but she said they couldn't afford to come now. This hurt me but I knew if they could, they would be there. I knew they were there in spirit and that they would be praying for me.

Patrick went by and picked up Mama Matae, so they could come to the graduation together. It would have been wonderful if my sister, Charlotte, and my two brothers, Tray and Bobby, could have come. They are scattered all over the world so I knew that wasn't possible.

After graduation, Patrick and some of the other graduates and I went out to eat. Mama Matea said she had rather go on home. She was too tired to hang out with us. The next day, Patrick had a dozen roses sent to my apartment. I was really surprised. He is a very thoughtful person. He seems to always say and do the right thing.

So many people have helped me – most of all my parents. They sacrifice their savings for me. I will repay them as soon as I can.

Mama called me to see how I was doing and how graduation went. I told her that there was no other feeling like it and when they called my name out to go across the stage – you couldn't touch me.

I am going home for a few days, I need a break. It will be so nice to be with my parents. Today is Thursday and I talked to Patrick last night about it and he said that he would see me before I leave. I called Clara, my supervisor, at work and told her that I would be back next week and we would work on my schedule then.

Patrick came and helped me put my things in the car. I went over and told Mama Matea goodbye. She begged me to drive careful and to hurry back. When it was time for me to go, I really hated to leave Patrick. He leaned in the car window and cupped my face in his hands and kissed me so tenderly. I really dreaded the drive home, but the further I got down the road the more I really knew that I just wanted to get there. I didn't want to stop for anything but about ten o'clock I was so tired I decided that I better stop. I found a small motel off the interstate. I have gotten a little braver since I had been living in New York. I went inside, paid for my room, got the key, and went to my room.

I got up early, excited about seeing Mama and Daddy. I hit the road with home on my mind! The drive went smoothly. My exit is right up ahead. Man is it hot or what?! June in the South is murder. Everything looks so good, green and alive. I guess I am just glad to be getting close to home. There is the house. When I turned into the driveway, I saw Mama at the door. She came running out waving with a smile on her face ear to ear. She held out her arms, "Gayle, my girl, look at you! Don't you look good?"

I hugged her so tight, "It is so good to be home. Mama, how are you? You look tired. Are you alright?"

"Come on in honey."

"Where is daddy?"

She pointed toward the bedroom. "Honey," she whispered. "He is not well, not well at all. Go on in and speak to him. Then we can talk. He is so happy that you are coming home."

I walked through the door and saw my daddy lying so still. I leaned over and kissed him on the cheek. "Daddy, how are you?" He opened his eyes, smiled, and closed them again. I felt the sting of hot tears running down my cheek. When I turned around, I saw Mama was also crying. We went into the kitchen and sat down at the table.

"Gayle, your daddy is a very sick man. The doctor doesn't give much hope. It is his heart and blood pressure."

"Mama, why didn't you tell me?"

"Honey, you were so far away and he insisted that we not tell you. He wanted you to do well and finish your school. He knew if you found out, you would come home. Don't be mad, it's just that we are so very proud of you and we didn't want anything to upset your plans to finish."

"Mama, I could never be angry with you. I love you even more for trying to protect me. Please tell me, was the Doctor sure about Daddy?"

"He said that he has congestive heart failure and a very hard blood pressure to control. The medication just doesn't help that much. Dr. Cathcart wanted to keep him in the hospital but he refused. He told the doctor that you were coming home and that you would take good care of him."

I called the Director of Nurses at the hospital where I worked and explained to her about my father. She told me that she would clear it with the hospital board. She felt sure they would understand and give me the time that I needed.

During the days to follow, we would take Daddy outside in his wheelchair. We would sit for hours under the big magnolia tree in front of the house. We talked about old times. It was wonderful. Sometimes he would drift off to sleep. I just sat beside him and watched him remembering what a wonderful father he has always been. Mama made some lemonade and came out to join us. She looks so tired today. She has lost weight but never complains about anything.

"I love you, Mama, so very much. Thank you for being such a great Mama all my life."

She smiled her sweet smile and sipped on her lemonade. "Child, you have always been such a sweet girl – never selfish, not like the other children. Bobby, Tray, and Charlotte were good in their own way but you always stuck right by our side. You know Bobby is still on a mission in the Far East. I haven't told him how sick his daddy is. I guess I need to be honest with all of them. Tray is still working as plant manager for that fertilizer plant in Rockford, Tennessee. He was home two weeks ago. Your daddy really did have fun with him. Tray likes to joke around and make your daddy laugh. He sure was happy about your schooling and graduation. He loves you a lot, you know?"

"Yes, he always took my side when there was an argument between Charlotte and me. How about her? Is she still enjoying the lawyer? What's his name? Jefferson something?"

"Yes, they seem happy. You know your sister. There always seems to be something wrong. She isn't an easy person to make happy. Never was." Mama touched me and pointed at Daddy.

I walked over to where he was. "Well, look who finally woke up. Are you hot out here?"

He nodded and said in his little weak voice, "Please take me inside, honey. I am so tired." I quickly took him into the house. Mama and I put him in bed. He didn't look well to me. I told Mama to call his Doctor. She agreed. The Doctor told us to call the ambulance and get him to the hospital. Mama began to cry. She is so afraid of losing him. I am really scared too.

FOUR

I SAT WITH DADDY while Mama got on the telephone. She called Tray and Charlotte. She tried to explain to them that they needed to come home. Charlotte lives in Biloxi, Mississippi. She said she would get home as fast as she could. She talked to Tray and he said he would catch the next flight out.

The ambulance came. They checked Daddy and hurried away with him. He looked so scared but he did not argue with us about leaving. We followed them to the hospital. In the Emergency Room, Dr. Carthcart said that he thought Daddy was having a heart attack. He would know how serious it is after some of the blood tests came back. They took him upstairs to the Intensive Care Unit. They asked us to go to the waiting room.

After about an hour had passed, the doctor came out and he told us it was a heart attack and that it was very serious. After the doctor left, I sat with Mama. We both cried and prayed that God would help him to come through this. We called the preacher from Mama's church, Paul Sicks. He came and went in to see Daddy. He said Daddy was glad to see him. He said a prayer with us and left.

Tray came in about five. He went into the unit. When he came out he sat by me. "Gayle, we are going to lose him aren't we?" He began as I nodded. I hated to admit it but things did look bad. We are worried about Mama, too. She needs to rest but won't leave.

Charlotte came in at eight o'clock. Mama went with her to see Daddy. Tray and I decided to get the Red Cross to try and locate Bobby. Tray called and told the woman that was working the phones about the situation and that we needed him at home as soon as possible. She was very nice. She got all the information about Bobby and assured him that she would start right away on finding him.

Being a nurse surely is not helping me. I feel so helpless. There is a little garden right outside the waiting room. Mama and Tray spend a lot of time out there. Charlotte and I have had a chance to renew our relationship. She seems to have mellowed out some. Maybe time and a good man has helped.

The telephone in the room rang, the attendant answered it and motioned for one of us. I went to answer it. It was Bobby. He was in Charleston, South Carolina. This is about an hour away or maybe two. He was going to try to rent a car and come to us as fast as he could. We didn't talk long, but I could tell that he was crying. He asked if Mama was alright. I told him we were holding on, but for him to please come fast, but to drive carefully. We did not need anything else to happen, not now.

I decided to go back in the unit to see if there was any change. He looks so weak. He tried to talk to me. I told him to just rest and try to feel better. The doctor has ordered medication to be given to him when it is needed to keep him calm. He knows what is going on. He is very smart. He held my hand when I kissed him on the cheek. I told him that Bobby was on his way. He turned his head toward me and smiled.

I went back out to where everyone was sitting. I told them that he had responded to me a little and that he was holding on for Bobby. We are all so tired. We eat the food from the hospital cafeteria. It's not too bad but I have eaten better. None of us wanted to leave to go get carry out. We have also washed off in the bathroom every morning. It will be alright maybe – we aren't too dirty. We actually laugh and joke around about it.

At about six thirty, Bobby came in. He ran over to us, "How is Daddy?"

Mama hugged him so tight. "Son, he is here and that's about all. You need to go in and see him."

Bobby hugged all of us and cried like a baby. We tried to comfort him. He went in to be with Daddy for a while. He said Daddy realized that he was here. We have all grown apart from each other during the past few years. It really feels good for all of us to be together.

Daddy lasted one more day after Bobby got home. It was as if he was determined to have all of us around him when he died. We were all in the room with him when he drew his last breath. But you know it was easy to let him go. He looked so peaceful. He didn't struggle at all. He just closed his eyes and went to be with God. Mama held his hand and we all just hugged her and each other.

The funeral was so beautifully done and the flowers were pretty. He would have loved them. There were a lot of their friends there. Mama and Daddy were very active in church all their married life.

After the funeral, Charlotte, Tray, and Bobby had to do what they thought was best. They all had responsibilities with work and all. Bobby had to go back to his job in the Middle East. I worry about that but he seems to like it. Charlotte went back to Mississippi, and Tray left for Tennessee. I stayed around for a while to make sure Mama was alright. She is so strong. She insisted that I go back to my apartment and go to work. She was never afraid to be by herself. She had lots of close neighbors that would be right there with her. I knew I needed to go back but it was so hard for me. We packed up all of Daddy's things and took them to a shelter for homeless people. We knew that Daddy would have liked that.

On Friday morning, I told Mama I really needed to start back to New York. I made her promise to keep in close touch with me. I could tell she hated to see me leave. I knew it would be alright. She is so strong. We just have to pray for each other.

Friday is here, I am packed and all my things are in the car. I decided to walk around the yard before I left. This is where I grew up, played with my dolls, and climbed this same old tree. The smell on honeysuckle was still in the air. It grew along the side of the yard. Mama kept the yard so neat. I think this is her passion. She loves flowers, really anything to do in the yard. Well I have to go. It's already getting hot and I have a very long trip ahead of me. Mama was standing on the porch. Saying goodbye was so hard. She looks so tired and sad. I hugged her tight and kissed her on the cheek.

She said, "Now Gayle, don't get all weepy. Just get in the car and go."

As I drove away slowly, I could see her standing on the steps waving. Of course, I cried my eyes out.

I decided to get some gas and a bite to eat before I get back on I-95. I stopped at a store that also had sandwiches. The girl fixed me a grilled chicken sandwich. I sat down to eat instead of trying to drive and eat. I will be so glad to see Patrick. He called me a few time, but I need to see and hug him! I think I will call him before I go much further.

FIVE

I COULD SEE A pay phone across the parking lot. I paid for my lunch and gas and walked to the telephone. I dug through my purse for some change. I dialed his work number. His secretary said that he had gone home early because he wasn't feeling well. She thought it was a stomach virus or something.

I tried to find some more change so I could call him, but I didn't have any. I went back inside the store to get change. I looked up and this dirty looking man was watching me. I sat down hoping that he would leave. He came over to me smiling. "Miss, I don't know you but I need to talk to you for just a minute." He seemed to be okay, but I was nervous.

"What do you want?" I asked as I sat back down at the table.

"I was told that you are a nurse. I need someone to listen and help me."

"Are you sick?"

"No, you see, my wife is real sick and we are very poor. Maybe you can come to the house just to see her. I promise it's the truth. We have an eight year old girl and she does all she can for her Mama. I have to work so hard helping people on their farms and stuff. I cannot be home until real late every day."

"I need you to tell me how you found me and how in the world you knew I was a nurse?"

He said he stopped at the country store down from my house. He met and talked to a man that knew me back at home. His name was Samuel something. He told him about his wife and about the face that he couldn't seem to get any help. This had to be Samuel Bethea. He was always at the house helping Daddy do things in the yard. He came to the house when Daddy died and I told him that I had gone to school and was a nurse now.

I asked him his name. He told me his name was Robert and his wife's name was Maryanne. His little girl's name was Ginny. "We live out that way," he pointed south toward the next town. "We live back off the road, kinda in the woods. Ginny can't go to school because she takes care of Maryanne. I know I am in lots of trouble about that but I don't know what else to do. I hope that you could maybe go and see her before you go away. We don't have any insurance or money to help us. The doctors don't give us much hope for her to live. They say she has cancer in her female organs and that it is spreading to other places too. I was just hoping you might know something I can do now. Maybe I was wrong. Sorry, I bothered you" he said as he turned and walked out the door. I got up and followed him out.

"Wait just a minute. I need to call my Mama and let her know what I am doing. Then I will follow you to your house."

I called Mama and tried to clue her in on what I was going to do. She had a fit and asked me if I was deranged, following some man I never heard of home. I convinced her that maybe God had put me in his path in order for me to help him. I don't know. I just feel like I need to do this. She told me to be careful and to call her.

I got in the car and followed him. I feel like I will be alright. He did say he met and talked to Samuel. Way down deep inside, I still feel a little nervous. We drove about ten or so miles and then we turned onto a dirt road. It's about three o'clock now. I don't want to be too late leaving. He pulled up in front of this little white house. I pulled in behind him. The yards were neat – maybe that was a good sign. He got out of the truck and came over to me. He could sense that I was nervous. "Please don't be afraid of us. We really mean you no harm." I felt a little more at ease.

We went inside. The house was a wreck. He led me to the living room. His wife was lying on the couch. She looked so pale. He told her who I was and that I was going to try to help them. Maryanne turned and looked at me. She tried to smile and spoke so softly I could barely hear her.

"Thank you for coming. I know you probably thought Robert was a demented man but we have tried to get help from different places but no one seems to care." Robert called his little girl into the room. She was dirty but you could see the beauty that was underneath it all. She didn't speak much but she slowly waved her little hand and went to the couch to her Mama. She laid her head over on her Mama and began to cry. Maryanne cried with her – how sad a picture this was. I knew God had sent me to these people. I had to help all that I could. They told Ginny that I was there to help. She stopped crying and smiled at me. I think she may have thought I came there to take her mother away from them.

I called Patrick and told him the story. He had a fit. He was afraid at first because I took Robert's word about Samuel and then the fact that I might have to stay overnight. This made him mad. I promised to be careful and to call him later.

I asked Ginny if she would let me help her take a bath. She was scared at first but Maryanne told her to go with me – that it was alright. We got through the bath okay. She actually seemed to warm up to me a little. She took me to her room. It was so small that only a single bed and a chair would fit in it. Her clothes were in boxes on the floor. I looked through them and found a little pink gown with a bear on the front. She put it on and actually let me brush her hair a little. She went and lay down beside her Mama on the couch. Maryanne thanked me for helping her bathe. She had been doing the best she could by herself. She didn't want her daddy to help – shy I guess.

I didn't feel afraid anymore. I could see that they were afraid of what was going to happen to them as Maryanne's sickness got worse. Robert told me that her cancer was probably all over her body. I told them that I would stay overnight and when morning came, I would get on the telephone and try to get them set up for home health care.

Robert had fixed fried chicken and potatoes for supper. I was hungry but I wondered how safe the food was – he was so dirty but he had worked all morning in the field. Maryanne ate very little. She was in a lot of pain. I helped her take her medicine and she soon fell asleep. Ginny ate real well. She had begun to trust me, I think.

Ginny soon went to bed. I went to the kitchen where Robert was cleaning up. "I am sorry the place is such a mess. I haven't had the heart to clean up. Maryanne requires so much help and I have really had my hands full." I told him that I would stay and help until I could get some constant help. He was so grateful that tears began to fill his eyes. They didn't have any family that lived nearby or any neighbors close by. I don't think they ever went to church either so they were really alone in their troubles.

I took this time to explain to him about how home health worked. He was afraid at first. I had to explain that it would not cost him anything. I think that when a social worker comes and sees the need, she can get help from the government. He was so relieved about the chance of that.

I slept in Ginny's room. The chair was big but I was not comfortable to say the least. I didn't sleep hardly any at all. I could hear Robert up with Maryanne. She seemed to be in constant pain. No wonder he looks so beat. I am surprised he isn't sick himself.

When I woke up, Ginny was sitting on the floor playing with a doll. I got up and went out to check on Maryanne. She was sitting on the side of the sofa, looking pale and tired. She told me that last night was the way she had been for months. I can't understand why the doctors haven't done something to help her.

Robert had coffee making on the stove. It smelled so good. I went in and spoke to him. He seemed to be a little more at ease this morning.

"Would you like some coffee?" he asked.

"Yes, I think I will have a cup. Can I fix Maryanne some?"

He told me that she would not drink it. She has so much nausea all the time. I think it is probably the pain and her condition together.

After breakfast, I helped Maryanne with her bath. She is so thin. I could see her bones. She wanted to go to the couch and lie down. Even with my help walking, she barely made it. She lay down and closed her eyes. She was completely exhausted from the bath.

I went into the kitchen and saw that Robert had cleaned it up. Even after staying up most of the night, he seemed more at ease. We sat down with Maryanne and talked about what needed to be done for them. She looked at Robert for reassurance. He smiled and told her that he agreed with me.

I called the agency that I found in the telephone book and explained to them what was wrong. The lady I talked to said they would send someone out to check them out. I didn't even know their last name and I had to get it for the paperwork. "My last name is Johnson. I'm sorry with all that has been going on, I really forgot."

The lady from the agency came out. I was glad because as soon as I could, I needed to get going. I waited to see what happened. They filled out all the paperwork and got Robert to sign them. She assured him that with the information she had gotten and their financial situation, they would qualify for a nurse to come out every other day to help them as long as she was needed. When she left, Robert told me that he could never thank me enough for the help and all the little things that I had done while I was there.

Ginny came out of her room wearing a cute little yellow dress. She came over and got in my lap. This really was a surprise. She had been so shy. She looked up at me with those big brown eyes, "Do you like my doll?"

"Yes, I sure do. What is her name?"

"Molly," she replied.

She got down and slowly went over and kissed her Mama on the cheek. Then she smiled at me and went back to her room.

SIX

I SAT AND TALKED with Maryanne and Robert for a while. They were so grateful for my help. It really made me very humble. I have never been faced with anything quite like this. I asked her if she was a Christian and she assured me that she was. She said that was the only way she was able to hang on with all the suffering she had been through. Robert said that he also believed in God. I told him that head knowledge would not save him. That he had to have heart knowledge also. He just looked at me. Maybe he will accept Jesus into his heart one day, I truly hope so. I went on to tell him how to be sure that he was going to heaven. He listened and thanked me for taking the time to tell him.

I told them that I had to go. It was eleven o'clock and I wanted to make some headway before it got too late. She pointed at a picture on the wall, "That's me when I was young and healthy. That's Ginny in my lap; she was about three months old." She was very pretty with fair skin, big blue eyes, and beautiful dark hair. I told her how pretty she was and that Ginny would probably grow up to be just as pretty as her Mama.

I hugged them goodbye. Ginny came over and hugged me – she is so cute. I gave them my address in New York. They promised to keep in touch. I felt like I would never see Ginny again. I probably won't see any of them really. They promised to call the school and get Ginny enrolled. She needs to get a good education. Maybe when she is older she will be able to help her Daddy more.

On down the road, I called Mama and Patrick to tell them I was on my way again. I feel like I have been in a dream world for days. I made several stops along the way. I am so tired. I finally stopped in Virginia and got a motel room. I really need to get some sleep. I have not slept well for the last few nights.

I got up early and was in a hurry to get going. The tripped seemed to take me forever. I guess I am ready to get back in my routine. I pray for Ginny. She is such a pretty little girl. I hope her Mama being so sick doesn't affect her emotional well-being. I pray that she will realize that there is a great big world out there, and that she can be a part of it in some great way. Her great smile and personality will take her a very long way if she will just realize what she as to offer.

Arriving at home was great! I don't really like to travel so far alone. I decided to go over and speak to Mama Matae before I went inside. I told her that we would sit down in a day or so and I would tell her all about my trip. I hurried back across the yard and got by stuff from the car. I ran upstairs and threw my luggage on the bed and called Patrick. He said that he couldn't wait to see me, and he would be over tonight. He sounded so glad to hear from me. It sure did feel good to hear his voice. I can't wait to see him. I feel like we have been apart forever. I called my Mama and told her I was home safe and sound. I thanked her for continuing to pray for me. I promised to write her a long letter and catch her up on everything.

That night when Patrick finally got to my apartment, we really enjoyed being together. I tried to remember everything that had happened since we were together. He held me tight, "Gayle, what if something had happened to you? What in the world would I do? I can't bear to think about that! We need to talk about something anyway."

"You look so serious. What's wrong?"

He smiled, "Nothing is wrong, but I am very serious. I know we haven't been together very long but I love you."

I really didn't expect this from him now but maybe the fact that we have been apart made him realize how much he cares for me. "Patrick, that's wonderful, but you know, I've just started a new job and maybe we shouldn't get too serious right now." I turned and looked at him. I have never felt such a rush before. His blue eyes were shining. He looked so nervous and before I knew it, I hugged him and said, "I love you, too."

He picked me up and swung me around and around. "Gayle, Gayle, I'm so happy! I just knew you loved me too!"

"Patrick, wait slow down please. We must take it easy. We shouldn't be in a rush. We need to be sure about what we are saying."

"Gayle, I'm not rushing into anything. I just know that I love you. I love you, Gayle!" He kissed me long and gentle.

"We are good together, that's for sure." I had to agree with him.

We sat and talked for a while. Patrick stood up and said he had better get going. It was ten o'clock and he had to get up early for work. After he left, I just sat down in shock. I am really in love with this great man! I have to settle down. I have a busy day tomorrow. I need to get my schedule at the hospital worked out.

I took a shower and soon went to bed. The moonlight gleamed across the bed. I could see the sky through the window. The stars were so bright and beautiful tonight. As I lay there, I had to thank God for my life and for all my different experiences. I feel like my life is on a roll so to speak. Things are looking up again. I have a good job and a wonderful man who loves me!

Morning came fast. The telephone woke me. It was Patrick and he was still on Cloud Nine. We talked for a while. He wants to get married soon. I think I need to work for a while first. We will have to talk about this some more. Right now, I must call the hospital and see when I go to work.

The supervisor told me I had one more day off. I was glad

because this would give me a chance to get my uniforms ironed and my mind refocused. I have been through so much these last few weeks: School, Daddy's death, and also going to a strange man's house. I'm not sorry about that though. I had to leave Mama and that was so hard to do. You know, through it all, I still thank God for it all. I think I am a stronger person because of it.

My first day back to work was a little scary. I felt overwhelmed with the responsibility but I did alright. As time passed, I learned to relax and enjoy what I was doing for the patients. I loved the little children. They were so sweet. As time passed, I enjoyed helping the older, sicker patients feel better. I would come home so tired but it was a really good feeling knowing that I made a small difference in someone's life.

Patrick and I have planned to get married. We are hoping maybe around the tenth of June, if it can fit in everyone's schedule. We see each other about twice a week. I have a very heavy schedule and he does too. We do manage to talk every night. He is a good Christian man and I am so blessed to have him in my life.

Patrick and I decided to go talk to my family about the plans for the wedding. The time is going by so fast. We asked Charlotte and Bobby to be in the wedding and they are so happy to do it. I wish Daddy was here to give me away. He will be missed. Mama has been so happy for us. She is such a great person and she is a wonderful Christian. I pray that I will be half the Christian she is.

Patrick and I decided to go see her on my next day off. They really get along well. They are both such good people. We enjoyed our time out there and we planned the wedding. I have decided to get married at home. I want Mama and all the people I grew up with to be there. The church I grew up in holds so many memories. Both of Patrick's parents are dead and he only has one brother, Michael. Michael lives in Virginia and he will be Patrick's best man. The two of them have grown close since their parents passed away.

SEVEN

WE WENT BACK TO New York. The trip really had us worn out by the time we got home. At least we could take turns driving.

The girls at work gave me a shower. I received so many nice things. I packed all of it up. I knew that we would be going home for the wedding in about two weeks. The time has really passed by fast. We stay so busy all the time. We can figure out what to do with all of it after the wedding. We will be staying at my place until we decide to build a house or not.

We leave for the Carolinas in the morning. I have already packed up most of my clothes for the wedding. By the way, the dress I decided on is so pretty. It has a short train, heart shaped neck line, and puffy sleeves. The neck has simulated pearls around it. I think Patrick will like it. I hope he will like it. We decided to drive his car. It has a lot more room in the trunk than mine. He has a very nice car – a black four door Lincoln.

Today we leave to go home. Patrick is on his way over here to load up my things. I hope he left some room in the truck. I not, maybe I can get it all in the back seat. We got everything in his car and I hope I haven't forgotten anything. We got on the road about nine thirty. We have not stopped but twice and I am getting tired. We took turns driving and this helped a lot. It's almost eight thirty and we are not far from Mama's house – thank goodness! Within the next hour, we will be there.

We drove into the yard. It feels so good to be home.

"Patrick, look Mama is standing on the porch and smiling from ear to ear!"

"Yeah, I think she is happy to see her girl."

"Mama, Mama," I yelled as we hugged each other.

"Patrick, you come over here son and let me have a big hug." Mama loves him like he was her own. They really get along well. I am so glad. We are a great family and hopefully it will stay that way.

Patrick unloaded the car and I found a place to put everything. By the time we were finished, Mama had fixed us something to eat. She had been busy cooking and there was a lot of food. She is expecting Bobby and Charlotte at any time now. It is getting late for Mama to be up. She usually goes to be fairly early.

Michael, Patrick's brother, is coming in also, but he and Patrick have a room at the motel uptown. We ate supper and enjoyed it. We fixed two plates and put them in the oven. I helped clean up the kitchen. Patrick went and sat in Daddy's chair. Mama and I just stood there and looked at him.

"Your Daddy would like Patrick," she said tearfully. We were both getting too emotional and had to change the subject.

Patrick and I walked outside. He had to go to the motel. It was time for Michael. "I love you, my almost wife."

"I love you, too, my almost husband," I replied.

We laughed and hugged each other. He drove away and I felt a little tearful. My thoughts went wild. I think the Devil is trying to get me upset. What if something happened to him? "Oh stop that!" I said out loud. We are both in God's hands and I want us to stay in His will. I refuse to let the Devil mess things up for us!

Mama and I lay across her bed and talked about the things we had been through. We enjoyed the quiet time together. She got up and went to the door. Charlotte was home and Bobby came in with her. We sat around the table together while they ate supper. We laughed and talked for a while. Mama said she had to go to bed. We kissed her good night. She went to her room and yelled down the hall, "Gayle, you sleep with me. Charlotte can sleep in your room and Bobby can have his room." I told her that we would settle down soon because we have a big day tomorrow. It felt good to sleep with Mama. It sure has been a long time since I have.

Morning came quickly and we had so much to do. Mama and the preacher's wife had done most of the decorating at the church. I put on jeans and a tee shirt and we all rode out to the church. "Mama it looks so pretty. Thank you." I kissed her cheek. Charlotte and I went to the front of the church. The ferns were so pretty. There was one on each side with big white bows on them. Mama's friend, Edna, sure does know how to tie bows. The first three rows had bows on the end of the aisle. Mama had really gone all out to make it look just right. She and Edna had saved me time and money.

Charlotte and I walked back through the front of the church. We talked about Daddy. It is still not real that he is not here. Charlotte asked me why I didn't have a ring. I told her Patrick and I had decided to have bands only. A diamond doesn't mean that much to me anyway, and we are thinking about saving for a house someday. Charlotte agreed that I was probably right and that we would need the money later.

We went to the kitchen and Mama said she was ready to go. On the way home, we talked about how much we missed Trey. He is doing secret things in the Far East. He seems to be happy and writes to Mama often but that's not the same as seeing him.

Mama said that she had forgotten to tell me that she had Samuel to plant a weeping willow tree in the back yard. She knew it was my favorite tree. "It's small now but it will grow. Gayle, when the wind blows, the little leaves shiver and sway. It is completely silent, it's soft like the voice of God. When you children think about it or see it, please remember your old mama said to listen quietly for the voice

35

of God, like a whisper in the wind. I am old now but I've seen a lot in my sixty-eight years. God will lead all of us if we let him, most of the time I want things to go my way, not His, and this not good."

When we got home, it was sunset. We all went to the backyard to see the tree. It was small but beautiful. I hope it will live and grow big. In time to come, we will all remember what Mama told us about it. We went inside. Mama and the ladies from the church had taken care of the finger food for the reception. I felt like I hadn't helped very much.

Time passed so fast. I slept with Mama again. I felt in my heart that this would be the last time. While she was sleeping, I slipped out and called Patrick. We talked for a long time. We are both excited about tomorrow. Our lives were about to change and never to be the same again. I could not sleep. I was too worked up about the big day! I got up and sat by myself in Daddy's chair. I leaned it back and closed by eyes. I think I actually slept a little bit.

The morning came quickly. We got up and ate breakfast. I was not very hungry due to the excitement. The wedding is at three this afternoon. I can't believe that it's finally here. The telephone rang. It was Patrick. "Hello there," he said. "Are you ready to marry me?"

"Of course I am," I replied. He told me he was going to be at the church about 2:15. Michael would be with him. We then said our goodbyes. I sat down on my bed and thanked God so much for sending him to me. I don't think they slept any at all. He said they talked most of the night.

Mama came into the room. She looked so pretty – like an angel. Her hair was turned white but it is a beautiful white. The dress she bought to wear looks good on her. It's sky blue with sheer sleeves and her shoes matched perfectly. "Mama, you look absolutely beautiful!" I turned and gave her a big hug. Charlotte's dress was cream colored with long sleeves. They were sheer, so not so hot. She really looked great. She has a cute figure anyway. We both wear size eight clothes. I doubt that I stay small. I like sweets too much.

I put on my dress. Mama and Charlotte helped me. It looks

good. I hope Patrick likes it. I hope I don't stumble. These shoes are high! I decided to wait until I get to church to put on my veil.

Bobby and I rode together to the church. Mama and Charlotte went in her car. We went to the back of the church. We got my veil fixed and did a last minute check of everybody. Bobby asked if we were ready. It is fifteen till three and we need to go to the front of the church. We walked around the side of the church. The ushers were at the door. We peeked in. Mama was seated on the front seat. Patrick and Michael were standing with Preacher Dan. Patrick was white as a sheet! I was scared myself. Charlotte went up the aisle. She looked so pretty. It was time for Bobby and I to go. He held me tight, "Gayle, don't worry I've got you. Take your time." Patrick looked so handsome. He looked at me and a big smile came over his face. When our eyes met, calmness swept over me. The ceremony went off without a hitch. We said our vows, kissed, and down the aisle we went. I don't think I have ever been happier than I am at this moment.

The reception was nice. We enjoy being with everyone. We took Mama to the side and talked a little. We were ready to leave. Charlotte and Bobby came over and hugged us goodbye. We thanked everyone for the gifts and for coming. I turned and threw my flowers over my head. One of the cute teenagers caught them. While we were running to the car, people were throwing bird seed at us. This was fun. We stopped at the car for a few more pictures. The car had writing all over it and cans tied to the back. I kissed Mama and Charlotte goodbye. Bobby came up and hugged Patrick and me. Michael came over and hugged the both of us. We got in the car. As we drove away, everyone was waving and some were blowing their car horns! This was better than I had dreamed it would be.

We went back to Mama's house. She was surprised to see us. We decided to change into something more comfortable before we left for Myrtle Beach. My dress was so big. I hated to ride that far in it. Patrick pulled out some jeans and a tee shirt. I scrambled through my luggage and found a pair of jeans also. We left as soon as we changed and told everyone goodbye again.

The beach was so pretty. It was almost dark outside. We are going to stay in an ocean front motel so that we can sit on the balcony and see the ocean. Patrick, being from the north, hasn't been to the ocean but a few times. We checked in the motel. We got our bags and went up to our room. We were on the sixth floor. The view was so pretty and the ocean was calm as it could be. We ordered up some supper and sat out on the balcony to eat. We stayed outside for a while and talked about our future together. Patrick put his arms around me and smiled. "Let's go inside." I agreed, we went to bed. He held me close and I felt so safe in his arms. I hope our love will always be this wonderful.

We only stayed for two days. We both needed to get back to work. I have been out so much lately and I really need to make up some days. Patrick said he was getting behind at work also. I really hated to leave. It is so beautiful here, hopefully we can come again in a year or so. The trip home was really long. I am driving and Patrick is asleep. We are almost home. I feel so blessed to have Patrick in my life. We made it home safely and took our bags upstairs. "Patrick, I sure am tired. Let's just go to bed." He agreed that we could unpack tomorrow after work. We both have to go in. I have to be at the hospital at seven and he has to be at work at nine. We slid into some shorts and a tee shirt and fell into bed. It feels so right with him by my side. I like to sleep in his arms. I feel so loved and safe.

The morning came fast. I jumped into the shower. He is still asleep. When I finished dressing, I woke him up to say goodbye. He hugged me tightly. "Take care of yourself today, I love you so much." I kissed him and out the door I went. I will grab something to eat later, I don't get hungry early in the morning.

Patrick called me during lunch to check in and let me know that he was doing great and that he missed me so much. He is so thoughtful and always puts me ahead of himself. My shift was finally over. I stopped and grabbed the mail on my way home. Mama had sent the pictures of the wedding. I can't wait to see them. I went ahead and opened them. They are all so good. We will pick out the best one and have it enlarged and framed. When I opened the door, I was surprised. Patrick had unpacked almost everything. There were a few things still on the sofa, but at least he did help. I changed into a pair of shorts and began to put up the clothes. When Patrick got home, he said he would fix us something to eat so I could finish my job with the clothes.

Time has passed, we are still on a very good schedule. We get to spend evenings together.

Mama Matea still comes over sometimes. Her health is not good at all, but she remains a great friend to us.

EIGHT

PATRICK AND I HAVE been married one year today. I decided to fix a nice supper for us. It doesn't seem like that long ago but it has been a great year for us. He came home with some roses for me. "Patrick, you are too sweet. I love them." I kissed him and hugged him tight.

"I love you, Gayle, so very much – more and more each day."

He like the supper. We ate early and spent some quiet time together. Mama call to wish us much happiness on this special day. She sounded so tired but assured me she was alright. We worried about her being alone all the time.

About three weeks has passed since that sweet phone call. Mama's preacher, Preacher Dan, called last night. He said that Mama wanted him to call me. She is not going to make it through the day. She has suffered a serious heart attack. I can't believe it – I am going to lose my Mama, too. "Oh God, please spare her if it's Your will. If not, please don't let her suffer." I prayed. I call the hospital and got some time off. Patrick did the same.

"Patrick, my Mama has always been my best friend my whole life. What will I do without her?"

"Honey, when my Mom died, I was so lost. With God's help, we can stand the pain. I am here, first as your husband, then as your friend."

We packed a few things and started out for home. I wanted to call the hospital, but to be honest, I am afraid of what they will tell me. It's four in the afternoon. We should get there around eleven tonight.

We pulled up at the hospital. I got out of the car, while Patrick went and parked it. I ran in. Preacher Dan was sitting on the sofa. He stood up when he saw me. "Gayle, honey, come over here and sit down."

"Please tell me, how is Mama?" Patrick came in and sat beside me.

Preacher Dan took my hand in his, "Your mama passed away about ten o'clock. She didn't suffer. She was alert right up to the last few minutes. She said to give you her love and prayers. She smiled and stopped breathing. I am so sorry that you didn't get here in time."

I laid my head over on Patrick and cried. Oh what a terrible feeling. Preacher Dan prayed with us and then left. We stayed until the funeral home people came and got her. We left and went to Mama's house. I have to call the rest of the family. I talked to Charlotte and Bobby this morning. They knew that she was very sick. Now I have to tell them that she is gone! This won't be easy to do. We all loved her so much. We will get word to Trey so that he might be able to make it home for the funeral.

We pulled up in the yard. The house looks so lonesome. It will never be the same again. It was sad staying there without her here with us. Charlotte said she would come tomorrow. Bobby said he would get home as soon as he could. It's so late. I think it will be best to wait until tomorrow to get in touch with Trey. I sure do hate for him to hear that she is dead with not knowing that she was so sick. We didn't sleep much at all. Patrick sure has stood right by me. He is a good man. We called the funeral home and asked when we should take the clothes up there. They were so nice and said to come when we were ready. We decided to go ahead and go. We made the arrangements for the funeral while we were there. Hopefully, Trey will be home by Sunday. That's three days away.

We called the Red Cross. They said they would get Trey as quick as they could. I know he will be shocked to get the news. I really hate for him to hear it from a stranger. Patrick went out and got us a sandwich for lunch. None of us felt like eating. I walked outside in the back yard. I can still hear Mama talking about the willow tree. It has grown a lot since we were home. It's so pretty when the soft breeze blows – it sways back and forth. When I went back inside, Patrick said that the lady from the Red Cross had called. She said that Trey would get home sometime on Saturday. We are so thankful for this. Charlotte and Bobby should be coming in anytime now. Patrick and I laid across Mama's bed for a while. It felt good to rest. I think I fell asleep. I got up when I heard Charlotte calling me. She couldn't believe Mama was gone. She cried and we sat and talked for a while. Patrick went outside. I think he felt like we needed time together. Charlotte made the comment that now Mama and Daddy were happy. They have each other in the presence of God. What could be better? Nothing.

Bobby got home at about 7. He flew to Columbia, rented a car, and then drove home. The night was long and none of us could go to be so we talked almost all night. Trey got home on Saturday around two o'clock in the afternoon. It was hard for him to take all that has happened in. It is unreal.

The funeral was beautiful. We felt like Mama's life preached her funeral. She was such a good Christian woman. She was a good neighbor to everyone. She worked in the church, helping with everything that happened there.

After everyone left the graveside, we stayed and looked at all her flowers. She would have been so pleased.

"Gayle," Trey said, "Mama and Daddy are together and I know they are happy. We must keep in touch and keep this little family together."

We all agreed. We knew it would be hard to do with us so spread apart like we are. We went home and cleaned out the refrigerator. We threw out everything. Charlotte is planning to stay for three or four days more. I think she is going to ask Samuel's wife to come and help her go through all the clothes and things. We are planning to donate all we can to Goodwill. They help so many people in need. Mama would be happy about that. She really liked to help others.

Bobby was going to stay the night with Charlotte but Patrick and I had to get going. It's two o'clock now, so if we leave in the next hour or so, we can stop in Virginia and spend the night. Before we left Sumter, we went by the graveyard. The flowers are still so pretty. It made me so sad to think that we would not be here to keep flowers on their grave. We will be coming back in about eight months. The lawyer said that he would have the will concerning the property and the house ready. As we left the church, I felt sad. I wonder what life has in store for Patrick and I. I know God is in control of our lives and we just have to trust in Him.

We got home without any problems. It felt so good to be back. We have to get our lives back on track. It will help to stay busy. We have started going to a young married class at church. We really like it. We have made some good friends there. We have been praying that the Lord will lead us into His service. The youth group met last night. Patrick and I were so touched when Preacher Bill, the leader, prayed. The Holy Spirit was like a mighty rushing wind over us. All of our friends noticed us. The joy we felt was indescribable. I felt such joy. I felt like our lives were going to take a new turn. We stayed after church and talked to the Preacher. He said that he felt that God was dealing with us. We told him that we had been talking about helping the needy and the homeless people. We felt led to do missions of some kind. We prayed together and left for home.

When we got there, I check the mailbox. There was a letter from Robert, the man I helped with his wife. It's been quite a while since I have heard from them. As I read the letter, great sadness came over me. He said Mary Anne had passed away six months ago. He said that he was sorry that it had taken him so long to let me know. He had been going through a lot. Jenny was having a very hard time believing that he mama was gone now. She is about five years old now and it will be so hard for him to work and care for her too. I will send them a note. I am so sorry for them.

Work is the same day after day. Sometimes I am actually bored. Patrick is getting restless at his job too. I think we need a change. We have been to a church nearby that has had a missionary and his wife speaking to them. They are from Virginia and are stationed in Brazil. They are home for a short visit. We are really excited after listening to their stories of helping so many people. Patrick and I want children before we get to old to really enjoy them but if we went into the mission field, would it be wise for us to have small children? We have so much to think about and to pray about.

Patrick is so tired today. He came in, kissed me, and laid down on the sofa. He went to sleep so fast. I am going to fix us a nice supper. Most of the time, we eat light at night. We don't want to gain too much weight. I would like to stay right where I am – 115 pounds. It's hard to do. Patrick weights about 189. He is tall and keeps away from sweets but not me – that's my weakness. Supper tonight will be great – fried chicken and creamed potatoes. I finished cooking and fixed the table real pretty. I went over to Patrick and kissed him on the cheek, "Hey you wake up. Aren't you hungry?"

He sat up, "Boy something sure does smell good. Girl you have been busy!"

After we ate, we talked and just enjoyed being together. We talked about going to the mission field and about not wanting time to slide by. Sometimes people have to wait for a long time before there is an opening. We talked about not wanting to have children-not at first anyway-and how there could be a lot of sickness wherever we might go. This is another area that we have decided to leave in God's hands.

We have read a lot about Romania. The people there are in such dire need of help. We saw pictures of some of the children. They were dirty and so skinny. Their life span isn't very long. I think they live to be about twelve or so years old. I don't know how the news peopled can go there and take pictures and hear all the sad stories. Then they just leave them. If I go, I won't leave them. Patrick and I talked at length about the children after we laid down to rest. Patrick soon drifted off to sleep but I could not shut off my mind. The moon is so bright tonight. Just think, some of the children over there never see it or it doesn't mean anything to them.

I awakened to the smell of breakfast. Patrick has fixed some eggs and bacon. I really like grits but seldom have them. Patrick doesn't care for them. He came into the bedroom and sat on the bed beside me. "Wow! You smell so good and so does the breakfast that you have made." I hugged him close.

"Well thank you my dear," he said with a big grin on his face.

"Patrick, we have a good marriage, don't we?"

"I should say we do, a very good one."

I got up and took a quick shower. Then we sat down and ate his good food. We dressed and went our separate ways to work.

At my work, I told my friend Martha about the news – things on TV that had my attention. She said that she had noticed that I was more quiet than usual. She thought maybe Patrick and I were having some trouble. I reassured her that we were just fine and that we were trying to decide to go to Bucharest on the mission field. She was so shocked, "Really, I would be scared to go to a foreign land. I guess I am not made for that sort of life." I told her that we had prayed for God to lead us and that this is the way we felt led to go. I hate to give up my job here but I have to follow my heart.

NINE

WHEN PATRICK GO HOME, he said that he had made some calls to find out the right procedure for us to follow. He had called a few places and finally he was directed to the Mission Board. He was told a lot of things we would have to do before they could consider using us. We have to get a lot of shots, get passports made, and then we can go to see them for an interview. They said sometimes they could place people right away and then sometimes it took a couple of months.

We got the shots, made the passports, and Patrick called them for an appointment. They gave us one on Friday at two in the afternoon. We will have to drive to Virginia, so we will need to plan to have that day off from work. We are so excited about this meeting. We went to the meeting. It was very interesting but it took about two hours. They asked so many questions about us. I think they just wanted to be sure that we are sure about going.

A week has passed and we expect to hear from the Board most any time. I think our visit went well, so maybe they will hurry up and find us a place to go. I wrote a letter to Bobby, Charlotte, and Trey. I want them to know what we are planning to do. I have mentioned it to them in the past but now we are serious about going. It's hard to get mail to Trey. It takes forever for him to receive it. He talked about all the political unrest in those foreign countries. He was afraid for our safety.

The Board called. We are going to Bucharest! This is what we have been praying for. Charlotte called me today. I told here where we were going. She was very emotional. She cried, "Gayle, I am very afraid for your safety. Are you and Patrick sure about this? I know you have talked about doing this for quite a while."

I told her that we had prayed about this and that we were sure. "Please, Charlotte, don't be afraid for us. We will keep in touch with you, Bobby, and Trey."

"I am so glad that I have a sister that is as dedicated to her beliefs as you are. When do you and Patrick leave?"

"We don't know yet. We have a lot of details to get straight first. I'll call you before we leave. Pray for us."

"I will and I love you."

I talked to the Administrator at work today. He was very nice and told me that he hated for me to leave but that he really admired me for going. Patrick was really giving up a wonderful job with a great future ahead of him but he never gave leaving a second thought.

The next couple of weeks passed by so slowly. The waiting is hard. Mama Matea was sad about us leaving. She feels like my real family. I will miss her. She has been like a real mama to both of us.

It is Monday. My day at work has been a very hectic one. It feels good to be home. I got the mail, went in, and changed my clothes. I decided to sit down and rest some before starting the laundry and supper. I picked up the mail and there were two letter – one from Robert and Jenny and the other is from the Mission Board. Oh, should I wait on Patrick to open it or not? I had better wait, if I can. I fixed a quick supper and waited for him. I read the letter from Robert and Jenny. He said they were doing well. Jenny talked about me a lot. She still remembers the time I was there with her. I will write to them when we get settled and tell them all the place we're at.

It hard to stay calm waiting on Patrick. I want to open the letter so bad! I hope its good news. Please God let it be.

"Patrick, you're home. Hurry over here. We have a letter from the Board. I have made myself wait on you to open it!" He pulled me down on the sofa beside him. He ripped open the letter and a huge grin came across his face. "Read it out loud!" I screamed. The letter read that we were to fly out from New York airport to Bucharest in two weeks. God, thank you, thank you! We laughed and cried for joy. We were so excited that we didn't get much sleep at all. The Mission Board send our tickets with the letter. They said they would have someone meet us at the airport in Belgrade. We would have to go to our living quarters on a bus. I can't believe all this is true!

I have a hard time concentrating at work. All I want to do is run around and tell everyone about my trip. Martha let me just rave on and on. She is a true friend to me and I will surely miss her.

When we got home today, I wanted to pack right away. Patrick assured me we had plenty of time. We decided to make some sandwiches and go to the park. The weather is nice in September. The afternoons are cool and sunsets are so beautiful. We went and he was right – it felt good to relax and talk. We need to start to let go of our ties here. We stayed in the park until the sun went down. We lay on our backs on a blanket and looked up at the stars. What a great sense of peace. We have had two great years here and made great friends and a lot of memories.

On our way home, Patrick was very quiet. When we got home, he went straight to the bathroom. I was unsettled by this time. When he came out, I asked him what was wrong, was he sick or something? He had tears in his eyes, "Honey, I'm not sick, I just feel unworthy of God's grace. He has granted us your inner most wish. I hope we won't let him down."

"Patrick, you are so dear to me. You are such a wonderful man." We hugged and each other and then we fell on our knees by the sofa and lifted our thanks to God for his blessings. I feel that we are truly in His will for our lives. We went to bed and finally drifted off to sleep.

The next morning, we got up early. I wanted to go next door and talked to Mama Matea. I wanted her to have time to get someone in the apartment as soon as we left. She depends on that income. While I walked over there, I started to think about happiness. There are so many different kinds. Patrick and I thought when we were married, that it was the greatest. Look at us now. God, I thank you so much for your guidance.

I knocked on the door. She opened it with a big smile on her face, "Gayle, come in dear."

"I can only stay a few minutes. I have to go to work and I wanted to tell you the great news. Patrick and I have received our appointment to go to Bucharest."

"Oh, that is so wonderful, honey! When do you leave?"

"We have two weeks to get everything ready."

She hugged me tight with tears in her eyes. "I sure will miss you both. You have been a blessing to me. I know you and Patrick will truly be blessed and be a blessing wherever life takes you."

I felt tears running down my face. "I must go or I will be late for work."

"Gayle, come back so we can talk some more."

I kissed her on the cheek and left. I felt a sadness for her. She is a lovely person.

The ride to work was wonderful. The sun was so bright and the trees so green. It feels like all is well with the world today.

When I got home from work, there was a letter from Mama's lawyer. He sent me a copy of her will. She and Daddy had left me a few acres of land at the farm. I had no idea what I will do with it. Well at least I will have a piece of my life from when I was growing up. Tray and Bobby got the rest of the land and Charlotte got the house. She always said she would like to return home to live one day. I guess I can let Charlotte rent out the land that is mine. At least it won't just lay out and grow up in weeds.

I put supper on. While I cooked, I decided to take a closer look at the paperwork on our trip and where we were going. The living conditions there are so different from here. We will have to really adjust to a lot of changes. We actually have been to a few meetings to understand how to approach the local people. We know we want to first tell them about Jesus Christ and how to be saved. I think we also have to be rejected by some. Their physical needs are so many. We will need to help with a lot of them at first. I love thinking about all the ways we can help. I put down the folder, turned off supper, and went on the porch to wait for Patrick to come home.

The trees are so pretty. Their golden leaves are shining in the sunlight. The sun is getting low. It's about five o'clock and the streets are very busy. Everyone is rushing home from work. I wonder what each of the families are talking about. It's really deep when we think about that. Every family has its own problems, joys, and goals. The little birds have built a nest in the tree beside my porch. They are so busy getting ready for their little babies. Maybe someday Patrick and I will have our own little babies.

"Gayle, what are you doing child?" It was Mama Matea. She was watching me while she watered her trees.

"Oh, I am waiting on that husband of mine to get home."

"That's nice. It is so pleasant outside today." She slowly walked over to me as her white hair gently moved with the breeze. She smiled all the time. I can't believe the first time I met her, I thought she was a very unfriendly person. She sat down beside me on the steps. "Honey, I can't tell you how much I am going to miss both of you. You have become like a daughter to me."

I reached and took her hand. It was pale and her skin was so soft and sweet. I think for the first time I realized that she was getting old now. She has been a very blessed lady. Her health has always been fairly good from what she tells me. We had been chatting for a while when Patrick drove up.

"What are you ladies up to?" Patrick asked smiling as he got out of the car.

"We are just catching up on everything. We have been talking about how much we will miss each other when we leave." Patrick leaned down and kissed me on the cheek and then sweetly turned and kissed Mama Matea also. She smiled. I could tell she really likes Patrick. He has never spent a lot of time with her, but she is so easy to love.

"Well, let me go home so you children can go ahead and have your supper." She slowly stood up. I invited her to stay and eat with us, but she said she had already eaten. We stood on the porch and watched her as she made her way across the yard. We will always lover her very much. She has been a very strong force in our lives. We may never see her again after we leave the states.

Patrick was tired. He had been training a new man to take his place at work. This had been extra work for him.

I have packed some of our clothes. That was a big job! I never knew we had so much to wear until now, but we can't take everything with us. There will not be anywhere to put all of it. Our living quarters will probably be only a couple of rooms. One of my fears is that the bugs and snakes will everywhere. I am so afraid of them!

Patrick fell asleep in the recliner. After I finished up the dishes from supper, I stretched out on the sofa. We are so blessed by God. Every day is new and we have another chance to do His will in our lives. We need to stop and love the more simple things of life – sunlight, the soft wind on our faces, and the way the rain smells. I could go on and on. I try not to take these things for granted.

Patrick looks so sweet just lying there. I slowly got up and lay down beside him. He turned over on his side facing me. He doesn't even know that I am laying here. It is really getting late and we need to go to bed. But I decided not to move from the comfort of being in his arms.

I awoke the next morning to find Patrick staring at me. "Hi. So you joined me last night, heh?"

"Well you looked so cute that I couldn't help myself." He hugged me so tight and kissed me so gently. "Patrick, we can't pursue this – even though I would really like to. It's six thirty and I'm off today, but guess who has to go to work."

"Yep, you are right." he grinned. "I will just have t rush home and pick up where we stopped."

While he took a shower, I fixed breakfast. He snuck up behind me, "Oh, you smell so good!" I laughed as he turned me around and kissed me.

"Patrick, behave yourself. Sit down and eat your breakfast." His big blue eyes shined as he smiled at me. I did well when I married him!

After he left for work, I cleaned the apartment and packed up a few more things. We have about eight days left here. I am so excited, but at the same time I am nervous about leaving the states. I hope my medical knowledge will allow me to help the young as well as the elderly people there. I think Patrick will be a lot of help to them. He has a great understanding of the <u>Bible</u>, and he is so smart business wise.

A knock at the door brought me back to reality. I opened it to find Mama Matea standing there. "I wanted to drop by for just a few minutes," she smiled.

"Come and sit down. I will fix us some coffee."

We sat and talked for a while. She handed me a gift. "What is this?"

"It's just a little something I thought you might like to have." I opened it to find a journal.

"Oh, this is so nice. We will enjoy writing down some of our thoughts and experiences." I hugged her. She stood up and said that she needed to go take her medicine.

She slowly walked across the yard to her house. She is a sweet, gentle person. I will always love her.

I ate a sandwich and lay down on the sofa for a while. I found myself counting my blessings. We have so much to thank God for.

Over time, I have learned so much about Patrick. He always amazes me and he is so strong-willed. He knows just what to say or do to make me feel better when I am down. After a short nap, I had to get supper fixed. It is almost time for Patrick to be home.

Patrick and I had a nice quiet evening. He said that he had a very hectic day at work. The new man he was training had been hard to work with. I might be Patrick. He wants everything a certain way and this can really get on your nerves sometimes.

We went to bed early and talked for a bit. He held me close. He smells so good. When we make love, it is so precious. We have so many great memories. He fell asleep fast but I am wide awake. My thoughts are running wild. Tomorrow is his last day at work and we leave on Friday – that is only two more days! I need to calm down and get some sleep. "God, I thank you for your grace and mercy. I pray that You will guide our steps wherever we go."

As the moon light twinkled throughout the room, it gave me the greatest sense of peace. I can't figure out how anyone can look at the beauty of the night sky and not know there is a God.

The night seemed to pass so fast. It was time to get Patrick up. I hugged him. He smiled. "Sweetie, it's time to hop up and get your shower. I will fix us some breakfast."

He was running around so happy that it is his last day at work. He finally went to the shower. I can't help but wonder how in the world a little country girl like me would ever get the chance to go and do the things that I am going to do.

After we ate, he kissed me goodbye. I sat down with my coffee and a book that I had been looking at on Bulgaria. It says that the people that live there speak Latin and only a few speak a little English. They grow wheat and maize. They also raise sheep. Yugoslavia joined with them to erect a huge plant at the Danube Gorge which harnesses the power of water rushing through the iron gate. This also will increase the road and railways through the Balkans. Bulgaria is very mountainous and rugged. The port at Varna is connected to the Black Sea. The farmers resisted the Communists takeover of their farms, but having only one port made them very, very poor. This is so interesting to read. I think it will help us to understand the way the people live.

We have stored everything except the thing we plan to take with us. I have to call the telephone and light companies. They will need to close our accounts. I probably need to call the water company, too.

I am going to the coffee house beside the hospital today. Some of the nurses I worked with want to meet and have lunch. I really feel sad thinking about probably never seeing them again.

We had a good lunch and talked about the good times we shared. They went together and got me a bracelet. It is so nice. It has crosses of all types and sizes. It is sterling silver – I will wear it forever! We promised to write and said our goodbyes.

Patrick and I need to call our families. I guess we can do that tonight. We were lucky – we found someone to buy the car. It seems weird to me, but we want need it. It is old and we won't get much for it, but every little bit helps.

TEN

IT IS FINALLY FRIDAY! We are rushing around getting ready to leave. We have to be at the airport at nine-thirty. The flight from New York leaves around ten thirty. "Patrick, at last we are leaving."

"Yep! We are out the door. I called a cab. It should be here in a minute."

We stood at the door and looked back in the house. We were both a little sad. We had been so happy here for a long time. The cab pulled up and the driver helped us load the luggage.

Mama Matea came across the yard to tell us goodbye. We cried but we were all happy. She watched and waved to us as long as she could see us. I pray that God will bless and keep her safe. I can feel my heart pounding with joy. We are finally on our way!

I enjoyed talking with my family last night. They were all so happy for us. Patrick called Michael. They really miss each other. Since their Mama passed away, they have really gotten close.

At the airport, the driver helped us with the bags again. He put them on a rolling cart. We went inside and got the tickets and headed off to find gate 134. The plane is really huge! American Airlines has a good safety record - that is what we have been told anyway. We boarded the plane. I took my seat by the window. Patrick asked if I was sure I wanted to sit there. He knows that I am afraid of heights. I told him I thought I would be alright. We buckled up and the plane began to roll onto the runway. In a matter of minutes, we were airborne! We held hands until the plane leveled off. I really hate to fly, but when you follow God's will, you want to do what is right. He will give you all the courage you need if you lean on Him.

There are a lot of people on the plane. We are going to Paris and I guess a lot of them are on vacation. I put my ear phones on and listened to some music. Patrick found a magazine to read. The stewardesses told us it would be a fairly long flight. The music made me sleepy so I made myself comfortable, put a pillow behind my head, and went to sleep. When I woke up, we were over the ocean. "Patrick, look! It's so beautiful and we are so high."

"The world is really spectacular." He smiled. "Honey, are you thirsty? The stewardesses brought some tea."

"Yes, that sounds great." I tasted the tea. It was really good. Sometimes it can be a little strong.

There are two children sitting behind us. They were with their Mama. They were playing and laughing – just as cute as could be.

The flight was smooth and very uneventful. The stewardesses announced that we were about twenty minutes away from the airport in Paris. "Paris! Wow! Who would have ever thought that me, a girl from a little town in South Carolina would be here?" Patrick smiled and agreed with me.

The plane landed at Charles De Gaulle Airport without a hitch. "Well, honey, how did you like the trip?"

"Patrick, I really enjoyed it very much." We went to the baggage rack and loaded the luggage on a cart and went outside and hailed a cab. We gave him the address to the Marriott Hotel which is not very far from here. This is a really big place. Everyone is running around speaking French. I can only understand a little but Patrick speaks French very well. Naturally, he did all the talking for us.

We arrived at the hotel and went to our room. We both fell across the bed. We were so tired. We rested for about an hour and then decided to venture out and see what Paris was really looks like. We also needed to find something to eat. The food on the plane was alright but not very filling.

We found a quaint little place called Castros. I'm not sure how to pronounce it, but the food was really good. The service was great and the people were nice and friendly. What we didn't finish, we brought back to the hotel with us. We watched TV and got ready for bed. It will feel so good to get some sleep. We ate some of the lemon pie we brought back from Castros. It was very sweet with whipped cream on top. It had nuts sprinkled over it. I was really too full to eat anything else, but I ate some anyway.

We watched a little bit more TV. I was too full to go to bed right now – I needed to let the pie settle down some. I really should not have eaten it! Patrick went on and lay down. I don't think he ate as much as I did. I love my sweets! I stayed up for about forty-five minutes. I turned off the TV and opened the blinds to let the moon light in. We are on the twelfth floor. I do not like to think about how high up we are but the view of the city is wonderful.

Patrick soon fell asleep. I guess he had some jet lag. I lay in bed thinking about Mama. If she could just see me now, I wonder what she would say. I hope she and Daddy would be proud and happy for us. I want her to know that I am still listening for the whisper in the wind like she taught me. I feel so much peace. I soon fell asleep.

We ordered a small breakfast up to the room. While we ate, we talked at length about getting some postcards and sending them back home to the hospital and our family.

We only had two days in Paris before we left. We tried to see as much of the country as we could. The days passed by so fast and here we go again packing up all our stuff. We tried not to buy very much while we were here. We do not have any extra room in our luggage. Who knows when we will ever come back this way? Maybe never!

The airport was so crowded. It is unreal how many people like to travel. We checked the schedule and we had about thirty minutes before our flight would leave. Patrick and I sat close to our gate so we wouldn't have to rush when it was time to board. This was another huge plane. It was a B-27 jet liner. We would stop in Rome, Italy, only long enough to change planes. I wish we would have time to look around. I remember studying Italy in school, but never thought I would ever see it!

They checked our passports again at the gate. This made me realize we were actually going into some unfriendly places. I asked God to surround us and to protect our journey.

The plane left on time. We are supposed to arrive in Bulgaria in about four hours. We had good first class seats. I sat by the window again. Well, it is ten AM in Paris. I don't know what the time difference is. Patrick held my hand as we lifted off the runway. I am still having trouble flying. I just have to place my trust in God. After we leveled off, we relaxed a little. Patrick settled back in his seat, "I think I might rest my eyes for a minute. Are you alright?" He smiled.

"Sure, honey, go ahead. I will be just fine." I lay my seat back a little.

I could see the beautiful clouds with the morning sun shining through. It was a clear day. The next few hours went by rather quickly. I think I actually dozed off myself. Before we knew it the pilot announced that we would be landing in about fifteen minutes. We were getting very excited. We were supposed to be met by a missionary by the name of Marc Stephens. I don't know how we will know him.

We landed at a very small airport. There were guards with very large dogs at the gate. They asked why we were here. We told them we were moving here from the states. They said something to each other and they all laughed. This made me uneasy. We went inside. Patrick told me to sit down and he would look around and try to find Marc.

The people were from a lot of different places. Their manner of dress was so different. The women wore long dresses and head scarves with no make-up at all. The air was so hot and dusty. Patrick walked around sill looking for Marc. This nice looking older gentleman walked up to him, "Are you Patrick?"

"Yes. Are you Marc?"

"Yes, you are correct." He asked us about our trip. We told him it was long and very tiring.

Patrick introduced him to me. "He Gayle," he smiled. "It is so nice to finally meet you two people." He made us feel at ease. He led us outside to his truck. It was old and shaky, but we climbed right in. He told us about the political unrest there, but where we would be was calm. We rode for about an hour. The roads were long and dusty. Marc told us his year there had been so rewarding. The people are so in need. The children are so eager to learn as well as some adults. Marc is French and English. His accent is so special. I love to listen to him talk.

We drove up to a small village and the children came running up to the truck. "Wait, Wait," Marc shouted. "Do not push. Let me tell you who these people are." The children all became very quiet and still. "This is Mrs. Gayle and Mr. Patrick. They have come a very long ways to help us." Marc spoke to them in Bulgarian with some English thrown in. "We must be kind to them. Okay?"

"Okay" the children chimed in unison. He said he had already told them we were coming. They were a very nervous people. The guns firing off in the distance made them so afraid. Their village has not had any fighting yet. They are about thirty minutes from the actual war.

Marc took us to our house. "This is your living quarters. It's not like America but you will get used to it in time." At that moment I think it really his us just how far we really are from home. We put our luggage in the house. Marc wanted us to go to the main house and meet some of the workers. We met Father HcHaney and two of the Sisters, Mary Kathryn and Sister Monic. They asked us to sit down and rest. They gave us some tea. The heat is horrible and is going to be hard to get used to. The room was very plain, but it was very clean. There were wooden table and the windows had shutters to cover them – not glass.

We sat and talked for a while. They told us a lot about the country. Bulgaria exports Alter of Rose which is an ingredient used in making perfume. They also grow maize and large amounts of winter wheat. They also raise sheep, but the children do most of the caring for them. The communists have taken over most of the ports. The farmers have resisted and only use the port at Varner. The people are so poor, sick, and afraid.

They told us many things that they hoped to accomplish with our help. We shared a small meal with them that consisted of bread, beans, and a little bit of rice. We had a very small piece of chicken – it wasn't fried, but it was good. We were hungry. After eating we thanked them for everything and left.

We went back down the hill to our house. It had a bed, a small sing, and a wooden table with two chairs. The only window is in the bedroom with no curtains or glass. The bathroom was very primitive. It consisted of a toilet and a very small tub. At least we did have a small stream of running water. There was a floor fan to use when we had to. The bed was clean. The nuns had done their best to make it as livable as possible.

We sat on the bed and just looked at each other. Patrick told me that we were going to be alright. Down deep inside, I knew that we would be. God never leads us down the wrong path so He will make things be right for us.

We slipped off our shoes and lay across the bed. It was getting dark outside now and a soft breeze was blowing. We can hear some of the children playing off in the distance. Their houses are down the hill from us, but since there is no other night sounds, we can hear them clearly. We soon settled down and went to bed. We were restless because it was so hot. The fan did give off a little air. I guess that is better than none at all.

We were awakened by the children at the door. I opened it and there stood little girls. They had picked some wild flowers and brought them to us. I thanked them. They smiled and giggled to each other. I asked their names. The taller one said her name was Shala. She was about eight. The smaller one said her name was Maria and that they were sisters. Sister Mary came to us across the yard, "Girls, do not bother these nice people." I reassured her that we were glad to have them for a visit. They made us feel welcome. Sister said for us to meet at the main house in about one hour.

We sat down with Father McHaney. We made plans for the next week. We shared a breakfast with only bread and a few small potatoes. They said they hardly ever got any meat or eggs. Marc reminded us that today is Sunday. It seems that we have lost a day or so. We prayed together around the table. This is very comforting to us. There is always strength in numbers.

We later went outside. There were benches set up for all of us to sit on. The people came from the village and sat down. They were there to listen to God's word. Father McHaney preached a very simple sermon. The people were very quiet and respectful too. Some of the adults stared at us. We have not had the time to meet many of them. After church was finished, we tried to talk to some of them, but they seemed reluctant to talk with us. The children ran around and were laughing and playing. I can remember my preached telling me one time, a day without laughter is a day wasted. This is so true. These children do not realize all the danger and fear that their parents know.

Monday morning I dressed in pants. I do not know how that will be accepted by the women. They wear dresses past their knees and scarves around their heads. I guess I will start out the day like this. We were told that the people would accept us in different attire so maybe we will be alright. Patrick wore his jeans. Most of the local men wore long pants too.

We went to the main house. I was going to work with the Nuns today. We were going to check with some of the families to see if there were any health problems. There was a doctor that came once a month. His name was Dr. Humonio, and he was to come today.

Patrick was going to down to the main part of the village with Marc to meet with some of the men. They were going to try to upgrade some of the farming and gardening. Patrick had studied about farming back in the states. He will be able to help them a lot.

During the next week, we worked very hard. The women seemed nervous at first but after about the third day, they calmed down a lot. I still get nervous at times. We really have to trust the nuns and the other people that are here. The times could get rough. I have to remember that God doesn't promise us a smooth journey through this life but a safe arrival in Heaven.

Most of the older women have bad skin and very bad teeth. Their personal health habits are as well as they know how to take care of themselves. There are two young girls pregnant. I really don't know about the fathers of the unborn babies. The girls are so hard to understand and I do not think they trust us very much yet. We have a great deal of trouble getting the people to come to the clinic.

It is very hard to get the supplies that we need to work with. We see a lot of diarrhea among the children and some of the tiny babies too. They get so sick. I wish we had a hospital. They need fluids so bad. There is a hospital about eighty miles away, but that is of no use to us.

Father McHaney has some friends in the city that would help get some supplies for us. The money to pay for this comes from a few good people that really love God and see the need that we have.

Marc is a very good man. He works with us every day. He speaks the local language and is well-known and trusted by the people here.

Patrick comes home every night so tired. He hardly has any appetite at all. We stay up late and go over our day with each other. I sat on the bed. Patrick came over, sat down, and laid his head in my lap. I stroked his hair, "Patrick, are you alright?"

"Yes," he smiled. "I guess I am just so tired. There were so many mosquitoes out there today. They really ate me alive!" I went down to the clinic and got a bottle of alcohol. He has very red and angry bites on his back and arms. The alcohol seemed to cool him down a little. "The men are eager to learn better ways to do things. Today, I actually spoke to two of them about their soul and told them about God. They were very attentive. Marc was there, too. He would help explain what they did not understand. I was so happy. I feel like I was really reaching them." I could tell Patrick was really excited about his day. We had come all this way to help the sick, but our main goal is to get their souls saved!

The water that we have to drink is supposed to be pure. It is bottled but the last shipment that we got really does smell odd. Dr. Hermonio fears that it may be contaminated. We heard that there had been a zinc spill down the river. This really worries me. Some of the people still drink from the river, even though we have tried to get wells built. We just haven't got nearly enough. The people are used to the river water, but not with zinc in it.

Dr. Hemonio decided to go down and get a sample of the water. He will mail it away to a lab to get tested. He said it could take a long time to hear from it. Meanwhile, we must try to reach as many if the people as we can. They have to be warned about this problem.

Patrick, Marc, and I walked down to the village. We went to the houses along the river first. I feel so sorry for them. Most of them still live in tents. This really breaks my heart.

Marc came up and started talking to us. "Now you and Patrick see what we are up against. The Serbs are treated very badly here. We get supplies sometimes, but not really enough to build a house. It takes about six months with everyone helping to buy boards, nails, and other things. These people really stick together and try to help each other."

I felt like my heart would break. All of the children are so thin and their eyes look so empty. I wish I could sit down with each child. I looked over at Patrick. He had tears streaming down his face. "Gayle, this is where God wants us. He has sent us on this very special mission. We must do all we can to change the lives of these poor people."

I asked Marc if we could stay for a while. He said that we could.

He went and got one of the boys that could speak some English. He also spoke the Serb language perfectly. He said his name was Helmyere and that he was sixteen. "Marc calls e Myere for short."

He was so helpful. A woman was lying on the floor. She looked so sick. I asked Myere to ask her what was wrong. She told him that she had not eaten anything all day. She pointed down at her little baby. She said the baby was sick also. I felt like the mother was severely dehydrated. If I can get some water in her then she might can let the baby nurse. I found a small container of water. It would have to be boiled before she could drink it. I asked Myere if there was something to cook on. He showed Patrick the tiny little stove. It needed wood to burn. Myere went out back of the tent. He soon returned with a few twigs. Patrick said he would do his best to get it hot enough to boil the water. The water was contaminated with different things. At least if we boiled it she would tolerate it better.

We stayed for a while. She ate some bread and drank two cups of water. We went into a few more tents. These people have so little. I wish the people back home could see this. These people would give anything to have just the crumbs from their tables.

We hated to leave, but we were so tired and tomorrow is a new day. Patrick knows how to put down a pump for fresh water. Maybe he and Marc can figure out a way. I don't know how the nuns have been able to care for all the people here. They do not seem to mind at all. I pray that Patrick and I can help out a lot.

On the way to the house, I told Patrick that I felt so guilty. Here we are going to a house, small as it is, but the people that we just saw only have a tent. They sleep on the ground with only a blanket under them.

When we got inside, we knelt down on our knees and prayed to God to lead and direct all our effort to help. We thanked him for sending us here. We need to remember every single day we open our eyes that God has given us another chance to get it right! Sometimes it takes us too long to wake up and see how blessed we are. I remember a statement that my Mama made years ago. She told me that sin was sneaky. She said that it could get into your life without you realizing it. She said it was like when you go into a dark room you can hardly see anything. Like sin it comes in slowly like light every day a little more. You become comfortable with the darkness. My Mama was a very wise woman!

The night was still and hot. Thank goodness for the little fan at the foot of the bed. Thank goodness for the generator up at the main house. Most of the time we can get enough electricity to barely run the fan. The moonlight spread across the room like a blanket. The same beautiful moon that I have looked at all my life. I was tired and sad. Last night Patrick slept without a tee shirt on and the mosquitoes bit him all over his back. The bites still look so red and swollen. He has been so uncomfortable.

Patrick woke up when I did. He sat on the side of the bed and got his Bible to read. I lay back down and watched him. He is so handsome. I feel so blessed to have him. He turned and smiled at me. "I saw you watching me."

"Is that so?" I jumped up and hugged him from behind. "Do you feel better?"

"Yes, my sweetheart. I think I do." His big blue eyes were so bright today. Maybe he is doing better.

"Let me see those bites on your back." He pulled up his shirt. "Yes, they are almost gone. I must be a good nurse after all."

He turned and hugged me. "I love you with all my heart, Gayle."

He is so sweet. He seems to know just what to say and when to say it. I hope the years will be good to us and we can be together for a very long time to come.

The days and weeks passed. The nuns and I visited as many of the tent people as we could every day. The elderly were dying at a rate of about one every two or three days. This is so sad, but they were so sick with malnutrition and unknown things. The nuns have done all they can with what they have to work with. When I was back home, I never dreamed that the need was so great here.

Patrick, Marc, and Myere worked along with some of the men

from the village. They had managed to put together another little house. The family that moved in was so grateful. They had come such a long, long way. They once lived practically outside. Then they moved to a tent and now a house with four walls and roof. To us this little house seems so small and simple, but to them, it is big and beautiful. I am ashamed I ever complained. I wish all of America could just be here for one day. Maybe they would send more money for supplies. I have my camera. I am going to take some pictures and send them back to our preacher at home. Maybe my home church will send help to us.

I sat at the table with Sister Mary. We shared some bread and rice along with some canned beans. We had bottled water and the food was really good. Maybe I am just hungry. I really miss some of the sweets like banana pudding or a good pie. I have always had a sweet tooth. The nuns never complained about anything. I need to be more like them I guess.

Patrick, Marc, and Father McHaney sat across the room planning the Bible Service. Sister Mary has taught a lot of the children some songs. We do not have any music, but the singing is so pretty. I know that God is well-pleased.

ELEVEN

WE HAD A WONDERFUL service tonight. Father McHaney
is so kind and loving. Our contact in the states sent a message. A
Baptist minister and his family from Kentucky have been assigned to
our area. This is wonderful! He has a God-loving family, a wife and
a twenty-one year old son. I surely hope they come to this village.

The nights seem to be getting somewhat cooler. It is the middle
of September. Maybe the cool weather is really on the way. It will
probably be here to stay. This concerns us. The winters here are so
cold.

Patrick and I helped straighten the room and said good night
to everyone. We talked about the cold weather on the way home.
Patrick tried to reassure me that Father McHaney surely had some
ideas on how to help the people survive the bitter cold. They do have
lots of blankets on hand. They are thing and ragged but better than
nothing. "If I remember right, it gets very cold here. We will have
to work fast to be ready."

We went to the house and sat on the bed. Patrick read his Bible
out loud. This always gives us peace - knowing that our wonderful
God is still in control. We dressed for bed and lay in each other's

arms. Patrick went to sleep as I lay there and listened to him breathe. Everything is so quiet here tonight. Only sounds are Patrick's breathing and the little clicking sound that the fan makes. Of course the mosquitoes are humming their heads off! We spray our rooms every day. The locals don't get sick from the bites like we do. I need to shut off my mind and go to sleep. I keep thinking about my family and wish I could see them. I do not hear from them very often.

Before I hardly knew it, it was morning. We got up and got going. The people are beginning to trust us more. I am so glad that the vaccine has arrived. I guess I will begin giving shots today. I hope they have sent enough syringes this time. "Patrick, what are you up to today?"

"Marc and I are putting together another house. We got started on it yesterday. I hope we have enough supplies to complete it."

"Well the doctor and I will probably be out in the village all day. We will give shots until the vaccine runs out." There is so much to do and not nearly enough help to do it all. I really hate going out in the wooded areas. The snakes grow very large here! I am so afraid of them but guess I had better get over it.

Sister Mary Kathern, the doctor, and I went down to the tent people. We gave shots to almost everyone. We tried to be sure the babies and the elderly got theirs first. Father McHaney met us on the way back to the main house. "Good news! Good news!" he shouted. "A plane is coming in with more supplies tomorrow." We are so happy. It is an answer to our prayers.

We are all so tired. At least the nights are beginning to cool off some so the bugs aren't as bad. We said good night, and walked down the hill to the house. The path going home is pretty dark and this makes me nervous. Patrick always teases me about being so afraid.

This became our routine for weeks on end. We are so tired we barely remember falling into bed. But it is a good tired. We are so blessed to be here and see the difference that can be made when we really try. God, I thank you for giving us this task to do. I pray that You will guide our paths.

The new preached and his family are arriving tomorrow. I hope we can work well together. We aren't sure if their son is coming with them or not. He is twenty-one years old. That might mean that he has other plans for his life. Marc asked Patrick and I to go with him to meet the plane. We drove about twenty-five miles through rough terrain to get there. At least the weather is cooler, but there is no help for all the dust that covers us.

"Marc, what are their names?"

"The pastor's name is Johnathan Lewis. His wife's name is Melody and their son's name is Jacob. You know they are from Bristol, Tennessee?"

"Yes. Father McHaney mentioned it to us."

We arrived at the airport before the plane got there. We walked around and spoke to some of the locals. They were there to unload the plane. We are expecting to receive more supplies today. "Look!" Patrick yelled as he pointed in the distance. "I can see the plane." Sure enough I could see it too.

"Man that sure is a huge plane." I think that Patrick is really excited that there is going to be another man that is young and able to help him work. Patrick is thirty-five and I am thirty-three. Maybe Melody and I will have something in common. The plane landed and Johnathan, Melody, and Jacob came down the ramp.

The wind was blowing sand everywhere. We all went to the plane to welcome them. Marc introduced them to us. Johnathan grasped Marc's hand and smiled. "Hello. Boy are we glad to be on the ground. The flight was really a rough one." Melody agreed with him. She said that she did not like to fly anyway and this flight surely did not change her mind. Jacob was very quiet but smiled a lot.

We helped get their luggage off the plane. While the locals took the supplies off and put them on the bus. We got on the bus and settled down for the long ride back. This will give us a chance to talk and get to know each other a little. Melody is a very tiny woman. She has long dark hair and dark eyes. Her son looks just like her.

Johnathan is tall and slender with light brown hair and big blue eyes. They make a very handsome family.

The country side must look strange to them. There is nothing but shrubs and lots of sand. I tried to reassure them that they would soon get used to the change. Patrick and Johnathan were just talking away with each other. Marc looked back at me. He smiled with a gleam in his eye. He seemed to sense that all would work out for good between us. Jacob stared out the window all the way back. He barely said a word. He may wish he had made a different decision about coming here.

We finally made it home. The children came running along beside the bus. They always get excited when someone comes. Patrick and I helped them with their luggage. We took them to their quarters. They would need to stay there until their house is finished. It has been built for about two weeks but getting the supplies to finish the inside has been very hard.

"Gayle, how long have you and Patrick been here?" Melody asked.

"It has been about a year, but it seems a lot longer sometimes. There is so much sickness and needs here. Along with all the suffering, we feel helpless sometimes. The weather does not help. Either it is hot and muggy or cold as ice." Melody looked overwhelmed. "Sorry, I don't mean to scare you. It is really worth it."

We got them settled in and introduced all the sisters to them. Jacob is so quiet. I told him about Myere and that they were about the same age. They would probably have a lot in common. He smiled. "Great! Where is he now?"

"Probably down at the bus helping to unload all the supplies. Patrick can take you down there so you can meet him."

Patrick looked at Jacob. "Sure, come along, Jacob; let's get over to the storage building. He will be there and he will be so glad to meet you."

When they left, I asked Johnathan and Melody if they wanted to go down to the village with me and meet some of the people. Patrick will come down later. They seemed eager to go with me. When we got down there, I could see the shocked looks on their faces. The people were happy to see them. They realized that the more help we had, the more help they would get. This had been a little bit hard for them. I assured them that everyday things would get better.

Jacob really likes Myere, but he admitted that he misses stuff from home – like TV and all his games. He didn't bring any of them with him because he figured if there is limited electricity, it would be a real problem trying to play them.

Time passed by and the new family seemed to do just fine. Johnathan really shared some great sermons. He really has the right touch. He can get a point across and you really do understand what he is trying to say. Jacob has started playing his guitar and singing along with his Mama. We all enjoy that so much. They are very talented people. When he plays music, the children get so happy that they being clapping their hands and dancing all around. We have been able to see a big change in Jacob. When he sees how much the music means to all of us, he just comes alive.

It's November now and we are getting ready for some very cold weather. We have to wear gloves and two pairs of sock to go outside. I am so glad Patrick and all the others that help have been able to get everyone off the ground and into small houses. They are very crowded but at least they are out of the tents now.

We have been able to get bottled water to everyone. The little babies are doing better now, too. They have clean water to drink. We also have dish detergent to wash out their bottles. We have some vitamins for them. Their mothers' milk was probably so weak that it didn't give them what they needed. We still get very little baby food so we have to make food for them that is soft enough for them to eat.

Birth control is absolutely unheard of here. We have tried to explain to the women all about other ways not to get pregnant. They cannot seem to understand at all. Maybe when their English gets better, we will be able to make them understand better. We can tell that they really want to learn. There are so many babies and no way to give them all the things they need right now.

We are trying to teach them all about Jesus and make them understand that He is what they need. The people here are mostly of the Muslim faith. This is instilled in them from birth. I really don't know a lot about that religion, but I think is makes it harder for them to accept Jesus. Sometime we all gather around the campfire and sing songs about Jesus. The children seem to really like that especially when Jacob plays his guitar. They have learned the song *Jesus Loves Me*. The adults are reluctant to try to learn. They do not like change. Father McHaney and the Sisters have gotten some of them to accept the Catholic faith. We try to meet their physical needs as well as their spiritual needs.

Myere and Jacob have become very close. They have a good connection with the young people. They have won several to Jesus Christ. That is why we are here – to save as many souls as we can.

It is Christmas time now and the people have heard the real Christmas story. Some of them would not come to any of the services we had. We tried to encourage them without pushing too hard. We do not have any decorations. We used some tree branches and a few little wild flowers. We can't find many – it is just too cold. We sang some Christmas songs and had the joy of knowing Jesus.

After Christmas, the time seemed to fly by. We are glad the weather seems to be warming up just a little. I was just thinking, it doesn't seem real that we have been over here for four years. It seems like every winter is colder than the last. I am really homesick. I hear from my family often, but I don't know when we will get to go home. Our assignment will be up at the end of this year. The states would look so good right now. We have accomplished a lot in the years that we have been here. Patrick and I have talked about maybe coming back over here sometime in the future. We will really have to pray for guidance about it.

Well we fussed about the cold weather and now it is getting hot again. We really need some rain. Thank goodness we have some wells down. Patrick and the guys have worked so hard to get us as much water as we need. We can take a sponge bath now; that's better than nothing. It would feel so good to take a long shower!

I am so glad that we have insect repellant now. Maybe we won't get sick from so many bites. "Gayle, come out here with me," Patrick called from the front porch.

"What's up?" He puts his arms around me.

"Sit down with me and look at the moon and all the stars." He was right. The moon was awesome and stars looked like they were so close to us. We talked about going home soon. Patrick is ready to go for a visit, too. It will be hard to leave everyone. We have all become close friends. We will miss the people also. The children are so sweet. We will really miss them!

Dr. Hermonio thinks his heart is about to put him down. We are really worried about him. He will soon be going home. I wonder who will take his place. He has been here longer than we have. I think the nuns said, about seven years. That is a long time to be away from your family.

Patrick and I decided to go inside. The bugs are beginning to crawl and it is time for snakes to crawl, too. I hope we never get bit by one. If someone does, we have the antidote for them.

It is July now and so hot. Father McHaney is very sick. We have been up with him almost all night. We are praying that God will spare his life. Dr. Hermonio thinks that he has had a heart attack. We do not have the right medication to treat him. He fought so hard to live, but about one o'clock this morning, he lost the battle. He will surely be missed. We cried and cried, but we know where his soul is. That helps with the heartache. Pastor Johnathan called the American Embassy. They said they would take care of all the details. His body will be sent to the States on Friday. Today is Thursday. His body will lay in the meeting room at the main house until they come for him.

When the morning came, a couple of us went down into the village to tell the people about his passing. They were very sad. He was loved by everyone.

The Consulate has found someone to take Father McHaney's place. He is really young. His name is Father James McPherson. He jumped right in and went to work. The nuns really like him. We can tell that he is a God-fearing man. That is a good thing!

October is here now and the weather is getting cold. The children like it – not so many bugs when they play outside. The new priest is settled in, but he talks about how much he misses the States. We know just how he feels. In time he will adjust. It is really had when you first get here. We all tried to help him. We remember how hard it was for us when we first came. God will give him peace if he will trust Him.

Patrick and I are going home. Patrick thinks that we need to leave before the snow starts falling. It is Sunday morning and Patrick is up and dressed early.

"Hey handsome, where are you going so early?"

"I thought I would go down to the main house and try to get a call through to the Embassy. I am so ready to go home, aren't you?"

"Yes, so hurry back with some good news." I ran and hugged him. "You have made me so happy!"

"Don't get too excited yet. It's not a done deal yet." He left and I sat down on the bed.

I know I need to go and check on the families down the hill, so I got up and left the house. One of the children had an elevated temperature. I went and told the doctor. He checked her and said that her throat was swollen and red. We have no supplied to do a culture here. He decided to send a blood sample to the hospital. This takes a while. We gave her aspirin and left some with her. The Doctor said he had some Penicillin and he would start her on some.

Patrick came in and he was so happy. "Gayle, we are going home."

"Patrick, that is wonderful news, but now we have a very sick little girl here. I hate to leave her until she is better." The Doctor insisted that we go ahead with our plans to go. He felt that she would be just fine. I could tell that this situation really got to Patrick. He is so tenderhearted especially when it comes to children. He asked her what her name was. Her mother said it was Sygeria. He assured her that we would be praying for her. She smiled and thanked him.

The children are so undernourished. I think that is one of the reasons they get sick so easily. We prayed for them and left. We have to get ready for our trip. We are leaving soon.

"Patrick, I am so excited. I know that I want get much sleep tonight. I want to go and I don't want to go."

"I feel the same way. We will be at home, but our thoughts will be here." He smiled and hugged me tight. "I love you, Lady" he smiled.

"You know what; I kind of love you, too."

We lay in each in each other's arms. The moon glistened across the room. We could hear the birds and other animals talking in their own language. We still have the utmost respect for all the animals that live here. Some of them can be vicious!

The morning was clear and cool. The weather is changing really fast. We talked about going down to the main house. Patrick went ahead and got dressed to go. I decided to stay and pack some. Dr. Hermonio came to the door. "Gayle, do want to come down the hill with me to check on Sygeria?"

"Yes, I sure do." I quickly stopped packing and grabbed a jacket. We left and went down the hill. The leaves were falling. We reached the house. I knocked on the door. Sygeria's mother opened the door. She was crying.

"Please come. She is doing badly." We rushed in. She looked much worse. We took her temperature. It was 104 degrees. The Doctor gave her a shot of penicillin. We bathed her with cool water. She was as red as she could be. The Doctor said that the blood reports had not come yet. He said we were only doctoring the symptoms. I could tell that he was very concerned. We checked her for any king of bite or sting. We didn't see anything. We sponged her down to cool her fever. She fell asleep. Her mother was so grateful. We went back to the main house. Patrick and Marc were going through the mail. "Did we get anything?"

"No. How is Sygeria doing?"

"She is still very sick. We hope the medicine will help soon." I sat down on the steps. I didn't know I was so dusty. The roads are dry and we need rain so badly.

"Gayle, we got a message from the Embassy. Our plane will be here around noon tomorrow."

"Oh, Patrick," I screamed with joy. "I need to go finish packing." I could see Melody's face. She looked sad. I know she doesn't want us to go, but she does understand.

On my way to the house, I passed Jacob. He was sitting on a tree stump playing his guitar. Myere was right beside him. Some of the children were these too.

Patrick soon came home. "Are you almost packed?"

"Not really. I don't know how much to take. We aren't going to be gone but about three weeks." Charlotte said she would have the house ready for us. She has been staying there for a while. I know I will miss Mama and Daddy so much. Charlotte said she would try to come over while we are home. Maybe I will get to see my brother also.

It is getting late so we went to bed. I could not sleep. Patrick slept hard. He was really tired. The sun woke me. I woke Patrick up and we got dressed. We sat down at the table and ate a bite. We asked Marc and Jacob to help us with the luggage.

When we got down the hill; Melody, Johnathan, and the nuns were waiting for us. We said our goodbyes and got on the bus. It was ten o'clock when we got to the airport. The big plane was there and some of the locals were unloading supplies. We got on board, waved to everyone, and buckled ourselves in.

The flight to Bulgaria was very tiring. A cargo plane is not very comfortable. We landed about twelve noon. The flight to Paris was almost ready to leave. We got our luggage and found a seat. Patrick decided to go get us a bite to eat. He got us a potato roll and some tea. The plane took off and we are on our way to Paris. I put Patrick by the window. Maybe this time I won't be so nervous. I held onto Patrick's arm while the plane was lifting off the runway. The plane leveled off and we settled down.

I sure hope the people we left behind will be alright. The flight seemed short. I guess I was day-dreaming. The announcement to put our seats upright brought me back to reality. Patrick looked out the window. "We are over Paris. I can see the airport," he leaned over and kissed me. "How's my best girl?"

"I am doing great!"

We got off the plane and went inside. Charles De Gaulle surely is big. We went down to gate 378. This is where we board for New York. We sat down across from a woman that had the cutest little girl with her. She smiled every time we looked at her.

We got on the plane for New York. I was packed. I think every seat was taken. This will be a very long flight. I can hardly wait to get home. I will see my sister. I hope Tray can be there, too. I really doubt that Bobby will be there. He is in the Far East and it will be very hard for him to get home. Maybe Patrick's brother, Michael, will be there. Patrick let him know that he would be coming through New York tomorrow. I wonder if I will have time to go by the hospital. It would be great to see Clara. We will probably stay overnight. That will give me time to visit.

I have the window seat this time. Patrick has his ear phones on and watching TV. I think I will take a nap. It will be wonderful to be home. I can hardly wait. I laid my seat back. I could hear soft whispers all around me. Patrick is asleep. He missed all of the movie he had started watching. He looks so sweet. I guess I love him to death!

I must have drifted off. The stewardess woke us up. We are coming into New York. We sat up and buckled up. We had a smooth landing. We are back in the good old USA! We got our bags and hailed a cab. The driver stopped at the Marriott Hotel. It looks nice. We got the luggage and went inside. It was very nice. We went up to our room. We were to wound-up to go to sleep. Patrick is so excited about seeing Michael.

The morning came fast, but at least we could stay in bed for a while. Patrick called room service and ordered us some breakfast.

"Patrick, we need to get in touch with Marc and the others. We need to check on Sygeria. I hope she is alright."

We are. It was good. We both dressed and went our separate ways. I am on the way to the hospital and he is on the way to see his brighter. Clara is still working and we have a really good visit.

When I got back to the hotel, Patrick was already there. He said Michael would be here in the morning. "He will call me so we can meet."

"You guys will have a ball catching up on everything. Maybe I will call Mama Matea. I would love to see her."

We went downstairs and found a deli. After stocking up on junk food, we went outside and found a table with an umbrella. The sky was so blue and the wind was blowing softly. We finished eating and took a walk. It was so much fun. When we got back to the hotel, it was dusk. The sky was lighting up in an array of colors. It is amazing what our God can do.

The night was quiet and very comfortable. We could not see the sky through the ceiling. This was really nice. I found myself thing about Jenny, the daughter of the man that me to his house. She is about thirteen by now. I wonder where they are. She was raised so hard and she was so young when her mother died.

When morning came, we had to stop and think where we were. We have decided to go and find Mama Matea. Michael won't be here until later. We dressed and called a cab. We pulled up to her house and asked the driver to wait and let us be sure that she was at home. She answered the door and we told the driver to go. We hugged and hugged. She looks so frail now and her body was so small. I went over to her kitchen window and looked at our old apartment. "It still looks good. I really liked living there." We talked for a while. We really enjoyed being with her. Patrick called a cab for us. We waited outside. When the cab arrived, we hugged our goodbyes and left.

We got back to the hotel around two o'clock and ordered some lunch. By the time we finish eating; Michael should be ready to meet with us. Patrick is so excited. He loves his brother so much.

We met Michael at a little coffee shop around the corner. We got there before he did and sat outside. The weather is so nice today. People were rushing around l. The place never changes. I think it only gets worse. Michael came running up to Patrick. "Hey, man!" he shouted. Patrick grabbed him. They hugged for a long time. He told Patrick that he had put on some weight but it really looked good. After a few hours, we asked him to come back to the hotel with us. He decided that he would. They stayed up late catching up. I excused myself and went to bed. Patrick came to bed about midnight and Michael went down the hall to his room.

We met him in the lobby around eight for breakfast. The time passed by fast. Michael had to leave for the airport. It was hard to say goodbye. Patrick hugged him again and he kissed me on the cheek. As the cab drove away, Patrick looked so sad, but he managed to smile anyway.

We went upstairs to our room. It was time for us to leave also. We had to pack and get ready to leave. We met our cab downstairs and went to the airport. We found our flight number. We had a few minutes before time to board the plane. We sat down close to our gate. They called our flight number and we boarded the plane. We sat near the wings. The plane was packed. We took off without a hitch and the flight was as smooth as could be. I lay back and took a nap. When I woke up, we were about to land. I sure am glad.

We decided to rent a car and drive home. It won't take long to get to Sumter from here. My sister is supposed to be at the house when we get there. I sure hope Tray can come. I do not expect Bobby to come.

We stopped in Charlotte, NC, and got a bite to eat. When we left I asked Patrick if he wanted me to drive for a while. He said that he was fine. Darkness came fast and the temperature was falling. We are at the exit to get off the interstate. We are about thirty minutes from my hometown of Sumter. It would be really small if it wasn't for Shaw Air Force Base. Charlotte will be so surprised to see us tonight. She is looking for us tomorrow.

When we drove up, she came running out screaming all the way to the car. I jumped out and we hugged and cried at the same time.

"Charlotte, you look so good. How did you do it?"

"Do what?"

"Get so skinny and pretty."

"You look good, too. Just as pretty as ever. Hey, Patrick, do you have a hug for me?"

He ran over and hugged her tight. We went inside.

"Charlotte, the house looks great! Mama would be so proud." We talked on and on. Patrick gave up and went to bed. We finally went also, but it was very late.

When we woke up, we could smell bacon cooking. Charlotte had fixed us a great breakfast. "Charlotte, you didn't have to do all this. Honey, I would have helped you." We sat down and ate. She wanted to know what I wanted to do today. I told her that I would like to go to the church and walk over the farm, too. I don't know if Patrick will want to come or not. He came slowly into the kitchen. He sat down and we ate.

When we finished, we all went for a walk around the farm. There surely are a lot of precious memories down here. The wind started to get cold, so we turned around and headed home. At the house, Charlotte gave us some mail that had come. It was Father McPherson. Everyone was doing alright and he spoke of how much they all missed us. He said the Sygeria was doing fine now. Melody, Johnathan, and Jacob were doing fine, too. The Sisters sent all their love along with Marc and Myere. We really miss them.

Patrick lay across the bed and we stayed in the dining room. We talked about our days here as children. We did not have much money, but we were happy. We have really enjoyed our stay. We have talked about our whole life, I think. Charlotte asked her friend from the bank to come over. He is really nice. He and Patrick hit is off right away. Charlotte said that Stephen is a very nice person. I think maybe she likes him.

Time is flying by so fast. I am glad we will be home for Christmas.

Charlotte and I have decided to go ahead and put up the decorations. We put up a big tree in the hall just like we did when we were little. The house looked so pretty. We asked Stephen to Christmas dinner. He came and we had so much fun.

We ate too much. We opened gifts. The days here have been wonderful, but tomorrow is Thursday. That means we have to get ready to leave.

I got everything packed and we will be leaving in a few minutes. Charlotte is so sad. So am I. But we have really had a great time.

The weather is getting bad. It's raining. I hate to travel in the rain. Patrick put everything in the car. We hugged and said our goodbyes to Charlotte. I cried and so did she. We waved as long as we could see each other.

Patrick was driving. It was raining so hard. I can hardly see anything. "Patrick, please slow down." Suddenly there was a loud crash and we were spinning around out of control. I could hear myself screaming Patrick's name and he was screaming out mine. When everything stopped, we had been sideswiped by a big truck. We were upside down in a field, "Oh, God, please help Patrick."

A man looked in my window. "Are you alright?"

"Yes, I think so. But my husband won't answer me."

"Try to be calm. The ambulance is on the way along with the fire truck. They will get you out and take care of your husband."

I was alright, but Patrick looks bad. He will not respond. They have him in the ambulance. I am going to ride with him. When we got to the hospital, I called Charlotte. She came as fast as she could.

They checked me out. I have a slight concussion, but I will be alright. I called Michael. I told him to come as fast as he could. I went in to see Patrick. He still does not respond to anything. "God, please don't take him from me."

The doctor came in and told us the he was not going to make it through this terrible ordeal. I felt my knees fold under me. Charlotte caught me and sat me in a chair.

"This cannot be true. Please do something for him." The doctor said he had no brain waves at all. I knew that was really bad. I wish Michael would hurry up and get here. We went in to see him.

I prayed for God to please help him. I lay my head on his chest. I could hear him breathing.

Charlotte screamed, "Look, his eyes are open! Look, Gayle!"

I looked and he was looking straight at me. I screamed for the doctor. Patrick put his hand on my back as he tried to talk to me. I kissed his swollen lips. He kept trying to say something. The doctor came in and said that he still had too many injuries to make it.

Patrick closed his eyes and we went back into the lobby. I did not want to leave him, but the doctor said that I needed to get still and quiet myself or I was going to be put into a bed. So we went and sat down.

Michael came running across the lobby. "Gayle, what in the world happened to you guys?"

I told him about the wreck and how bad Patrick was hurt. He went in to see him. When he came out, he was crying. "He looks so bad. What does the doctor say?"

I told him that Patrick was not going to make it. He had a fit!

We sat out there way over into the night. At about three in the morning, the doctor came out and told us that he was gone. I could not believe it. I ran into the room. I hugged him but he didn't move and he wasn't breathing. Michael and Charlotte came in with me. Oh what a terrible night it had turned into.

I looked at the peace that Patrick had on his face. I knew that he was in the arms of God.

I talked to Michael. I knew we had to make some decisions about what funeral home to use and where to bury him. We decided to put him in the same grave yard as my Mama and Daddy. This was alright with Michael.

The funeral was beautiful, but I still can't believe he is gone. After staying at the house in Sumter, I have decided to go back to Bosnia. I know that Patrick would like that.

In time, I got everything together. I have come back to the

people that really need me. I miss Patrick, but I know that he would be happy that I am here. We have a new nurse coming in today. I am so glad because we badly need the help.

On of the nuns came and got me. "You must come and meet the new nurse." I went with her and to my surprise; the nurse was Jenny, the little girl from back home. Her daddy was the man in the green truck that asked me to please help his wife that was so sick. Jenny was so young then.

"Mrs. Gayle, you will never know how your kindness to my Mama and to me changed my life. Even though I was very young then, I knew I wanted to be like you. I kept up with you and decided I wanted to be a missionary, too." I hugged here tight. I know that God's hand had been in this all along.

The years have passed. Jenny and I are still together helping the needy. I plan to stay. This is where God wants me.

I hope that everyone that reads this story will be moved to get out of their comfort zone and help someone that is in need.

RUTH INMAN

Printed in the United States
By Bookmasters